# Coping
# Skills
# Interventions
## for Children
## and Adolescents

# Coping
# Skills
# Interventions
## for Children
## and Adolescents

## Susan G. Forman

Jossey-Bass Publishers · San Francisco

For sales outside the United States, contact Maxwell Macmillan
International Publishing Group, 866 Third Avenue, New York,
New York 10022.

Manufactured in the United States of America

 The paper used in this book is acid-free and meets the
State of California requirements for recycled paper
(50 percent recycled waste, including 10 percent
postconsumer waste), which are the strictest guidelines
for recycled paper currently in use in the United States.

**Library of Congress Cataloging-in-Publication Data**

Forman, Susan G.
   Coping skills interventions for children and adolescents / Susan
G. Forman.
      p.   cm.—(Jossey-Bass social and behavioral science series)
(Jossey-Bass education series)
   Includes bibliographical references (p.  ) and index.
   ISBN 1-55542-493-7
   1. Students—Psychology.  2. Stress in children.  3. Stress
management.  4. Adjustment (Psychology)  I. Title.  II. Series,
III. Series: Jossey-Bass education series.
LB1117.F59    1993
371.8′01′9—dc20                         92-25004
                                                   CIP

FIRST EDITION
*HB Printing*   10 9 8 7 6 5 4 3 2                *Code 9294*

A joint publication in
The Jossey-Bass
Social and Behavioral Science Series
and
The Jossey-Bass Education Series

Consulting Editors
*Psychoeducational Interventions:*
*Guidebooks for School Practitioners*

Charles A. Maher
*Rutgers University*

Joseph E. Zins
*University of Cincinnati*

*To my parents
and
James D. McKinney, my professional "parent"*

# Contents

# Preface

Children and adolescents encounter a variety of potentially stressful situations on a daily basis. These events may involve family members, peers, or teachers; they may result from failure to achieve goals, or from physical illness or disability. Stress has been conceptualized as an interaction between an individual and the environment in which there is a stimulus or stressor, a response, and intervening variables consisting of personal characteristics of the individual. A sizable body of literature indicates that inability to handle potentially stressful situations or stressors may result in emotional, behavioral, and/or physical health problems.

Personal characteristics of the child or adolescent that mediate between the stressor and the stress reaction include skills that may be used to respond to or cope with a potential stressor. These coping skills consist of sets of information and learned behaviors that are purposefully used to bring about positive outcomes in potentially stressful situations. The learned behaviors may be physiological, social, cognitive, and/or affective.

The schools provide an appropriate setting in which coping skills may be taught either by special services professionals or by classroom teachers who have received specific training. The development of coping skills is directly related to the basic mission of the schools, which is to prepare youth to function effectively in society. Use of coping skills can prevent or reduce a variety of child and adolescent academic, emotional, behavioral, and health problems, and can thereby assist in the development of youth who are able to deal competently with a range of academic, interpersonal, and physical demands.

## Overview of the Contents

This book presents a number of intervention approaches to teaching coping skills to children and adolescents in school settings. The interventions focus on the development of a repertoire of physiological, social, cognitive, and affective responses that can be purposefully used in reaction to potential stressors. These skills can form the basis of individual competence in dealing with a wide range of daily demands and major life events. As such, the book should be of interest and value to a variety of mental health professionals working in the schools—school psychologists, counselors, and school social workers, as well as health educators, school nurses, and special and regular classroom teachers.

Chapter One provides an overview of approaches to defining stress and a description of the types of stressors children and adolescents confront. The role of coping in mediating between the stressor and the stress reaction is discussed, and the development of coping skills is presented as a means of enhancing competence in dealing with daily stressors and stressful life events.

Subsequent chapters present a range of interventions that have been developed and empirically evaluated; these techniques teach children and adolescents physiological, social, cognitive, affective, and behavioral coping skills that can be used to deal with potential stressors. The interventions are based on behavioral and cognitive-behavioral therapeutic procedures. Chapters Two through Ten each focus on a specific type of coping skills intervention, providing information on the historical development of the intervention, the procedures that make up the intervention program, special assessment techniques that are used in evaluating student change and the effectiveness of the intervention, and a review of the empirical research related to the effectiveness of the intervention.

Chapter Two discusses relaxation training. This intervention teaches children and adolescents methods of controlling their physiological responses in potentially stressful situations. It has been found useful in dealing with stressors that typically produce anxiety responses.

Chapters Three, Four, and Five focus on coping skills interventions that teach children and adolescents methods to deal with social stressors. Chapter Three details social problem-solving training. This intervention teaches how to cope with social problem situations through a structured sequence of cognitive activity. Chapter Four presents social skills training. This intervention remediates skill or performance deficits in interpersonal verbal and nonverbal behaviors. Chapter Five addresses assertiveness training, a specific type of social skills training that teaches individuals to express their thoughts, feelings, and beliefs in direct, honest, and appropriate ways without violating the rights of others.

Chapters Six, Seven, Eight, and Nine address coping skills interventions that emphasize emotional and behavioral control through cognitive activity. Chapter Six describes self-instruction training. This intervention teaches children to deal with a variety of potentially stressful situations by using verbal self-instructions to control their behavior. Chapter Seven focuses on rational-emotive therapy and rational-emotive education procedures. These procedures are based on the idea that thoughts and beliefs have a direct influence on emotions and behavior; they provide children and adolescents with methods of eliminating irrational beliefs and developing rational, constructive patterns of thinking.

Stress inoculation training is presented in Chapter Eight. This is a cognitive-behavioral intervention that helps individuals cope with stressors by increasing their understanding of the nature of stress, building a variety of cognitive and behavioral coping skills, and providing structured opportunities for skill rehearsal. In Chapter Nine, attribution retraining is described. This intervention helps children and adolescents develop beliefs regarding causes of success and failure that will have a positive effect on their future reactions to success and failure situations.

Chapter Ten describes behavioral self-management training. This coping skills intervention teaches children and adolescents to use behavior modification techniques to control their behavior, achieve their goals, and/or address their behavioral or emotional problems. Behavioral self-management skills can also be used to incorporate coping skills into an individual's behavioral repertoire.

In addition to providing a way to approach existing problems resulting from the inability to cope effectively, coping skills interventions can help children and adolescents to develop skills that will prevent the occurrence of emotional, behavioral, academic, and health problems. Chapter Eleven addresses prevention applications—coping skills interventions that seek to prevent alcohol and other drug abuse, negative effects of adolescent sexual behavior including pregnancy and sexually transmitted diseases, adolescent suicide, and disorders resulting from the experience of a disaster. Coping skills interventions are also presented as a way to promote general emotional and social competence.

Finally, Chapter Twelve addresses a number of issues that must be considered if coping skills interventions are to be implemented successfully in school settings. The organizational structure and processes of schools require approval and support from a number of sources; there must be specific attention to programming for generalization and maintenance of behavior change as well as for monitoring and evaluation of intervention effectiveness. Attention to these issues plus knowledge of intervention procedures and evaluative literature are essential for building competence in dealing with interpersonal, emotional, academic, and physical demands.

*New Brunswick, New Jersey*                         Susan G. Forman
*September 1992*

# The Author

Susan G. Forman is vice president for undergraduate education at Rutgers, The State University of New Jersey. Prior to assuming her current position, she was associate provost and professor of psychology at the University of South Carolina. She received her B.A. degree (1969) from the University of Rhode Island in psychology, her M.S. degree (1971) from the University of Rhode Island in school psychology, and her Ph.D. degree (1975) from the University of North Carolina, Chapel Hill, in school psychology.

Forman's research has focused on the efficacy of behavioral and cognitive-behavioral interventions with children and adolescents, and on organizational interventions in educational settings. She has been the recipient of approximately $1 million in research funds from the National Institute on Drug Abuse to investigate the effectiveness of coping skills training in the prevention of adolescent substance abuse. In 1984 she was elected to fellow status in the American Psychological Association. Her published works include approximately fifty journal articles and book chapters as well as a number of edited books and monographs, including *A Behavioral Approach to Education of Children and Youth* (1987, with C. A. Maher) and *School-Based Affective and Social Interventions* (1987). Forman has served on the executive boards of the National Association of School Psychologists and the School Psychology Division of the American Psychological Association.

# Coping
# Skills
# Interventions
## for Children
## and Adolescents

*One*

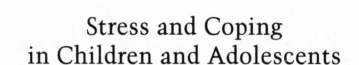

# Stress and Coping in Children and Adolescents

Stress, a constant of modern life, affects children and adolescents as well as adults. This chapter defines stress and begins exploring the importance of interventions for children and adolescents in mediating the effects of stress in their lives.

## Definition of Stress

Thousands of articles on stress have appeared in the professional and popular literature. Despite or perhaps because of this proliferation, a number of divergent definitions of stress have been developed, at times causing confusion in the field. A review of the stress literature reveals three major definitions of stress currently in use: (1) a stimulus-based definition, (2) a response-based definition, and (3) a transactional definition.

### Stimulus-Based Definition

Stimulus-based definitions of stress focus on the individual's experience of particular types of situations. Stress is seen as a strain on the individual caused by stimuli in the environment. Researchers using this approach have attempted to identify environmental events that disrupt normal activity, may be noxious, or place excessive demands on the individual (Holmes & Rahe, 1967). These events include (1) major changes, often disasters, which affect large numbers of people (such as earthquakes, hurricanes); (2) major changes affecting one or a few persons (such as the death of a significant other); and (3) daily hassles (such as feeling lonely, failing an exam). According to this definition, children experiencing major life events, such as their parents' divorce, or frequent unpleasant events, such as being picked on at school, would be seen as experiencing stress.

Compas (1987b) contends that both external and internal events can be sources of stress. External sources include a range of environmental stimuli such as family, school, or neighborhood events or conditions. Internal sources include physiological changes or development (for example, diseases, handicapping conditions, puberty). Compas (1987b) also distinguishes between acute and chronic demands. Chronic demands are enduring aspects of the social and/or physical environment that continuously create threats or challenges and typically involve deprivation or disadvantage. These would include physical disabilities, diseases, poverty, or a family in which repeated physical conflicts occur. Acute stressors involve changes or disruptions in existing conditions such as divorce, death in the family, or changing schools.

Thus, stress can be defined in terms of environmental or internal stimuli or situations that affect the individual. The more of these situations the individual experiences, the greater will be his or her level of stress. The major limitation of viewing stress as a result of stimuli is that this approach fails to account for individual differences in the perception of and ability to deal with potential stressors.

### Response-Based Definition

Response-based approaches view stress in terms of the individual's biological or psychological responses to a stressful situation. Hans Selye (1974), one of the major proponents of this approach, defines stress as the nonspecific biological reaction of the body to any environmental demand. These demands or stressors result in the disruption of a balanced state within the body, which may lead to a variety of biological changes. Selye contends that these biological changes represent objective indicators of stress; thus stress should be assessed by considering the individual's response to the environment. For example, stress in a child may be inferred because of observed anxiety or depression, or physical illness associated with the experiencing of adverse situations (such as complaining of headaches on school days). This definition is problematic because a specific response may not be an invariant indicator of stress.

### Transactional Definition

The most comprehensive approach to the definition and study of stress conceptualizes stress in terms of transactions or interactions between the person and the environment. This approach was developed by Richard Lazarus (1966), who proposed that stress refers to a stimulus or stressor, a response, and intervening variables. Stressors are viewed as having the potential for differential effects across individuals. The individual's perception of the environmental demand as a threat and the response capability of the individual to cope with this demand will determine the effects of a stressor.

This approach emphasizes cognitive-mediational processes. An event or stressor will be stressful only if the individual perceives it to be. In contrast to the previous two approaches, which view the individual as automatically responding to environmental changes, the transactional definition emphasizes the active role of the individual in mediating potential stressors in the environment. This definition of stress draws from both stimulus- and response-based definitions but goes beyond these definitions by focusing on intervening variables that consist of personal characteristics of the individual, and by emphasizing the transactional nature of the stress phenomenon. For example, student A and student B may have to present an oral report in their English class. Student A may perceive this task as one that will be difficult for him, that he will not do well, that will cause him to become anxious, and that will bring his grades down. His response may be debilitating anxiety. Student B may perceive the task as just one more hurdle that can be overcome with some effort and as something that, although somewhat unpleasant, can be dealt with through preparation. Her response to the same situation would probably involve only a minor amount of anxiety and a generally constructive approach to the assignment.

The transactional approach to stress involves the concepts of threat, appraisal, and coping. Stress results from experiencing an event that is perceived as threatening or that exceeds the ability of the individual to cope.

The concept of appraisal is an important aspect of the stress process. Lazarus and Folkman (1984) indicate that appraisal is a cognitive process through which individuals evaluate a potential stressor in terms of its significance for their well-being. They differentiate two types of appraisal: primary appraisal and secondary appraisal. Through primary appraisal the individual evaluates the threat value of a situation. A situation can be appraised as irrelevant, benign-positive (likely to lead to a desirable outcome), or stressful. If a situation is deemed stressful, it can then be further appraised as already having resulted in significant harm or loss, as being likely to have a negative impact in the future, or as a challenge with the potential for gain or growth. Through secondary appraisal, the resources available for dealing with stressful situations are evaluated. Coping options are appraised.

For example, Sally will be taking a basic skills exit exam next week. She must pass it in order to get a high school diploma. Through the process of primary appraisal she may view the situation as benign-positive because she is sure she will pass, or as stressful because she thinks the test may be very difficult for her. Through secondary appraisal she may determine that a helpful strategy could be to mentally rehearse feeling calm while taking the test, or she may think that she has no way of coping with the situation.

## Causes and Assessment of Stress
## in Children and Adolescents

Causes of stress or potential stressors have been defined by some as the experiencing of change and by others more specifically as the experiencing of negative events. Researchers appear to agree that these changes or events have a cumulative effect; that is, increased numbers of stressful events experienced within a relatively short period of time compound the effects of these events and make coping more difficult.

The Life Events Record, developed by Coddington (1972a), is an assessment instrument consisting of a list of events that were judged to be experienced frequently by children and adolescents. In developing this scale, Coddington compiled an event list and asked teachers, pediatricians, and mental health workers to rate each event according to the amount of social readjustment it required. Preschool, elementary school, junior high, and high school versions were developed. The event "birth of a sibling" was arbitrarily given a value of 500 and other events were to be rated above or below this value depending on the perceived degree of readjustment required. From these ratings, average readjustment ratings were computed and life change units were determined by dividing the average rating by ten. This scale yields a total life stress score by adding change units. Table 1.1 gives examples of events and their life change units for the various age levels. From the life changes of a sample of normal children, Coddington (1972b) has obtained data that can be used to determine whether a child is experiencing events more stressful than is typical for his or her normal peers. These data show that children tend to experience a greater number of life change units with increasing age, peaking at about age sixteen.

Johnson and McCutcheon (1980) attempted to improve on the Coddington (1972a) scale with the Life Events Checklist. Items for this were chosen from four sources: (1) the Coddington scale, (2) adult scales that seemed to be relevant for children and adolescents, (3) the authors' experiences with children and adolescents, and (4) an open-ended survey of forty-four black and white children and adolescents from varying socioeconomic groups who were asked to list the five most stressful events experienced during the previous year. These sources produced forty-six items, the first reflecting events over which the child has little control and the remaining items reflecting events that may serve as stressors but that are potentially under the control of the child. The events are shown in Exhibit 1.1. Ratings of these events produce a positive life change score, a negative life change score, and a total life change score.

**Table 1.1. Events and Life Change Units for the Coddington Life Events Record for Four Age Groups.**

| Life Events | Life Change Units | | | |
| --- | --- | --- | --- | --- |
| | Pre-school | Elementary | Junior High | Senior High |
| Beginning nursery school, first grade, or high school | 42 | 46 | 45 | 42 |
| Change to a different school | 33 | 46 | 52 | 56 |
| Birth or adoption of a brother or sister | 50 | 50 | 50 | 50 |
| Brother or sister leaving home | 39 | 36 | 33 | 37 |
| Hospitalization of brother or sister | 37 | 41 | 44 | 41 |
| Death of brother or sister | 59 | 68 | 71 | 68 |
| Change of father's occupation requiring increased absence from home | 36 | 45 | 42 | 38 |
| Loss of job by parent | 23 | 38 | 48 | 46 |
| Marital separation of parents | 74 | 78 | 77 | 69 |
| Divorce of parents | 78 | 84 | 84 | 77 |
| Hospitalization of parent (serious illness) | 51 | 55 | 54 | 55 |
| Death of parent | 89 | 91 | 94 | 87 |
| Death of grandparent | 30 | 38 | 35 | 36 |
| Marriage of parent to stepparent | 62 | 65 | 63 | 63 |
| Jail sentence of parent for 30 days or less | 34 | 44 | 50 | 53 |
| Jail sentence of parent for 1 year or more | 67 | 67 | 76 | 75 |
| Addition of third adult to family | 39 | 41 | 34 | 34 |
| Change in parent's financial status | 21 | 29 | 40 | 45 |
| Mother beginning work | 47 | 44 | 36 | 26 |
| Decrease in number of arguments between parents | 21 | 25 | 29 | 27 |
| Increase in number of arguments between parents | 44 | 51 | 48 | 46 |
| Decrease in number of arguments with parents | 22 | 27 | 29 | 26 |
| Increase in number of arguments with parents | 39 | 47 | 46 | 47 |
| Discovery of being an adopted child | 33 | 52 | 70 | 64 |
| Acquiring a visible deformity | 52 | 69 | 83 | 81 |

**Table 1.1. Events and Life Change Units for the Coddington
Life Events Record for Four Age Groups, Cont'd.**

| | Life Change Units | | | |
| Life Events | Pre-school | Elementary | Junior High | Senior High |
|---|---|---|---|---|
| Having visible congenital deformity | 39 | 60 | 70 | 62 |
| Hospitalization of yourself (child) | 59 | 62 | 59 | 58 |
| Change in acceptance by peers | 38 | 51 | 68 | 67 |
| Outstanding personal achievement | 23 | 39 | 45 | 46 |
| Death of a close friend (child's friend) | 38 | 53 | 65 | 63 |
| Failure of a year in school | | 57 | 62 | 56 |
| Suspension from school | | 46 | 54 | 50 |
| Pregnancy of an unwed teenage sister | | 36 | 60 | 64 |
| Becoming involved with drugs or alcohol | | 61 | 70 | 76 |
| Becoming a member of a church/synagogue | | 25 | 28 | 31 |

*Source:* Heisel, Ream, Raitz, Rappaport, & Coddington, 1973, 119–123.

The Adolescent Perceived Events Scale (APES) (Compas, Davis, & Forsythe, 1985), containing items identified by adolescents, provides a more extensive range of life events, including major life changes, daily hassles, and daily pleasures. This scale was developed partly as a reaction to the earlier adult-generated event lists.

The authors felt that the views of adults might not accurately reflect the views of children and adolescents concerning stressors. In addition, previous measures focused on major life events, although research with adults had indicated a strong relationship between daily stress and physiological and psychological symptoms (Compas, Davis, Forsythe, & Wagner, 1987). Six hundred fifty-eight adolescents between the ages of twelve and twenty were asked to provide a list of daily and major life events, either positive or negative, that had occurred in their lives in the past six months (Compas, Davis, & Forsythe, 1985). In addition, they were asked to list events they anticipated would happen in the next six months. The

**Exhibit 1.1. Events from the Life Events Checklist.**

1. Moving to a new home
2. New brother or sister
3. Changing to new school
4. Serious illness or injury of family member
5. Parents divorced
6. Increased number of arguments between parents
7. Mother or father lost job
8. Death of a family member
9. Parents separated
10. Death of a close friend
11. Increased absence of parent from the home
12. Brother or sister leaving home
13. Serious illness or injury of close friend
14. Parent getting into trouble with law
15. Parent getting a new job
16. New stepmother or stepfather
17. Parent going to jail
18. Change in parents' financial status
19. Trouble with brother or sister
20. Special recognition for good grades
21. Joining a new club
22. Losing a close friend
23. Decrease in number of arguments with parents
24. Male: girlfriend getting pregnant
25. Female: getting pregnant
26. Losing a job
27. Making the honor role
28. Getting your own car
29. New boyfriend/girlfriend
30. Failing a grade
31. Increase in number of arguments with parents
32. Getting a job of your own
33. Getting into trouble with police
34. Major personal illness or injury
35. Breaking up with boyfriend/girlfriend
36. Making up with boyfriend/girlfriend
37. Trouble with teacher
38. Male: girlfriend having abortion
39. Female: having abortion
40. Failing to make an athletic team
41. Being suspended from school
42. Making failing grades on report card
43. Making an athletic team
44. Trouble with classmates
45. Special recognition for athletic performance
46. Getting put in jail

*Source:* Adapted from Johnson & McCutcheon, 1980.

survey resulted in 213 nonredundant events, 148 of which were not included in existing measures of adolescent life events. Examples of these are shown in Exhibit 1.2. Three forms of the APES were developed. For young adolescents (ages 12–14), events are rated according to desirability. For middle (ages 15–17) and older (ages 18–20) adolescents, events are rated on their desirability and impact. This measure provides the most comprehensive listing of stressful events for adolescents to date.

The school environment has been recognized as a major source of potential stressors for children and adolescents because it provides a context in which performance and relationship demands are made (Forman & O'Malley, 1984, 1985). Two major categories of school stressors have been identified: (1) achievement stressors related to mastery of academic subject matter and evaluation of

**Exhibit 1.2. Examples of Events Identified by Adolescents Not Included in Prior Adolescent Life Event Measures.**

*Major Events*

Graduation from junior or senior high school
Moving away from parents' home
Friend having emotional problems
Parents discover something you do not want them to know
Change in birth control use
Brother or sister getting separated or divorced

*Daily Hassles and Pleasures*

Taking care of younger brothers or sisters
Change in privileges or responsibilities at home
Arguments or problems with boyfriend/girlfriend
Not getting enough sleep
People interrupting you when you are trying to get work done
School interfering with other activities
Getting punished by parents
Feeling pressured by friends
Going to parties, dances, or concerts
Pressures or expectations by parents
Car trouble
Homework or studying

*Source:* Compas, B. E., Davis, G. E., & Forsythe, J. (1985). Characteristics of life events during adolescence. *American Journal of Community Psychology, 13,* 677–691.

performance and (2) social stressors related to social relationships with peers, interaction with teachers, and participation in classroom activities (Phillips, 1978).

## Effects of Stress on Children and Adolescents

Numerous studies have examined the relationship between child and adolescent stress and psychological and physical health. In general, however, most of these studies have been correlational in nature. Thus, although the physical and psychological health variables examined have been found to be correlates of stress (occurring at the same time as stress), in most cases causality cannot be implied. That is, we can conclude that a number of childhood and adolescent conditions occur concurrently with stress although we cannot definitively state that these conditions are effects of or causes of stress, or that stress is a cause of or effect of the condition.

### *Physical Health*

The onset of a number of health problems has been found to be related to life stress in children and adolescents. Life stress has been related to number of visits to the doctor, reports of diagnosed illness, self-reports of physical health problems, and days of school missed because of illness (Gad & Johnson, 1980; Johnson & McCutcheon, 1980).

Specific illnesses linked to stressful life events include streptococcal infections (Meyer & Haggerty, 1962), rheumatoid arthritis, appendicitis (Heisel, Ream, Raitz, Rappaport, & Coddington, 1973), recurrent abdominal pain, chest pain, and headaches (Greene, Walker, Hickson, & Thompson, 1985; Hodges, Kline, Barbero, & Flanery, 1984; Pantell & Goodman, 1983), respiratory illness (Boyce et al., 1973), childhood cancer (Jacobs & Charles, 1980), and juvenile-onset diabetes (Leaverton, White, McCormick, Smith, & Sheikholislam, 1980; Stein & Charles, 1971). In addition, exacerbation of chronic illness during childhood and adolescence has been linked to the occurrence of stressful life events. These illnesses include juvenile-onset diabetes (Brand, Johnson, & Johnson, 1986; Chase & Jackson, 1981), asthma (Bedell, Giordani, Amour, Tavormina, & Boll, 1977), and cystic fibrosis (Patterson & McCubbin, 1983; Smith, Gad, & O'Grady, 1983), as well as hemorrhaging in hemophiliacs (Heisel et al., 1973). Life stress has also been linked to accidental injuries (Beautrais, Fergusson, & Shannon, 1982; Coddington & Troxell, 1980; Padilla, Rohsenow, & Bergman, 1976) in general as well as in sports-related situations.

## *Psychological Health*

Psychological and behavioral problems in children and adolescents have also been linked with life stress. Overall level of psychiatric symptomatology has been related to life stress as well as specific psychological problems and constructs such as anxiety, depression, poor self-esteem, external locus of control (Barrera, 1981; Johnson, 1986; Lawrence & Russ, 1985), substance use (Wills, 1986), anorexia nervosa (Strober, 1984), and suicidal behavior (Cohen-Sandler, Berman, & King, 1982). In addition, life stress has been linked to poor school performance for both elementary (Cowen, Weissberg, & Guare, 1984; Sterling, Cowen, Weissberg, Lotyczewski, & Boike, 1985) and high school students (Fontana & Dovidio, 1984).

## Coping and Coping Skills

Coping can be viewed as a set of responses, cognitive or behavioral, that people use to deal with problematic events (Lazarus & Launier, 1978) and to avoid being harmed by life strains (Pearlin & Schooler, 1978). Thus, coping refers to a set of purposeful individual reactions to stressors. It is a reaction to a stressor that resolves, reduces, or replaces the negative stressful state (Kagan, 1983). It is the process through which the individual manages the demands of person-environment relationships that are appraised as stressful along with their accompanying emotions (Lazarus & Folkman, 1984). These definitions assume that individuals are actively responsive to forces that impinge upon them. Compas (1987a) contends that the moderate correlations found between stressful life events and child and adolescent disorders indicate that individual differences in coping may buffer the relationship between stressors and disorders.

A number of authors have defined and explained the concept of coping in more detail. Lazarus and Folkman (1984) have identified six major areas from which people draw in order to cope:

1.  *Health and energy.* Important resources because an individual who is sick or tired has less energy than a healthy person to expend on coping.
2.  *Positive beliefs.* Viewing oneself positively and believing that life outcomes are controllable and will be positive.
3.  *Problem-solving skills.* The ability to search for information, generate alternative courses of action, weigh alternatives with respect to outcome, and select and implement an appropriate plan of action.
4.  *Social skills.* The ability to communicate and behave with others in ways that are socially appropriate and effective.
5.  *Social support.* Emotional, informational, and/or tangible support from other people.
6.  *Material resources.* Money and the goods and services money can buy.

Pearlin and Schooler (1978) indicate that people use social resources, psychological resources, and specific coping responses in dealing with stress. They define resources as what is available to people in developing their coping repertoires. Social resources are interpersonal networks that are potential sources of support. Psychological resources are the personality characteristics that people draw on to help them withstand potential stressors. Among the more important of these with regard to stress and coping are self-esteem, self-denigration, and mastery. Self-esteem refers to the degree that one's attitude toward himself or herself is positive; self-denigration refers to the negativeness of this attitude. Mastery represents the extent to which individuals think their lives are under their own control.

Pearlin and Schooler (1978) further define specific coping responses as the behaviors, cognitions, and perceptions in which people engage when dealing with their life problems. These may be influenced by psychological resources but are independent of them. The authors have identified three types of coping responses: (1)

responses aimed at altering the source of stress and changing the situation out of which the potentially stressful experience arises, (2) responses that control the meaning of a potentially stressful situation after it occurs but before the emergence of a stress reaction, and (3) responses that control stress after it emerges.

Compas (1987b) distinguishes between coping resources, coping styles, and specific coping strategies. Coping resources are defined as aspects of the self (for example, problem-solving skills or self-esteem) and the social environment (for example, the availability of social support) that facilitate dealing with stress. Coping styles are methods of coping consistently used by individuals across different situations or over time within a given situation—tendencies to react in a particular way in response to a specific set of circumstances. For example, Diane may try to think of positive aspects of any situation that at first appears to be a setback, such as not making a sports team or not being placed in a program for gifted students. Specific coping strategies are the behavioral or cognitive actions taken during a particular stressful event. For instance, Ken may do some deep breathing before he starts his English exam.

Compas (1987b) also points out that certain special characteristics of children and adolescents need to be considered when one applies to them ideas about coping that were originally developed based on adult functioning. First, children are dependent on adults for many basic needs; thus the child's social context is important in understanding his or her coping resources, styles, and efforts. Childhood coping is also dependent on personal factors such as temperament, or the child's sensitivity to the environment. Some children seem to be more predisposed than others to react with arousal or distress to a wider variety of situations. Thus, they may need to cope with a greater number of situations than children who are not predisposed in this manner. Finally, the child's cognitive and social development will influence what is experienced as stressful and how the child copes with stressors.

Folkman and Lazarus (1980) have described two major types of coping efforts: problem-focused coping and emotion-focused coping. Problem-focused coping efforts are those intended to act on the stressor; they include problem solving or attempts to alter the stressful relationship between the individual and the environment.

These efforts are directed at managing or altering the problem causing the distress. Emotion-focused efforts are those intended to regulate emotional states associated with the stressor, such as cognitive reframing (thinking about the stressor differently), use of selective attention (perhaps attending to positive aspects of the situation), or relaxation. Thus, this type of coping is directed at regulating emotional response to a problem.

In a study of 130 older children and young adolescents (ages 10–14), Compas, Malcarne, and Fondacaro (1988) found that both problem- and emotion-focused coping strategies were used in response to academic and interpersonal stressors. Use of emotion-focused strategies increased with age for this sample. In addition, the researchers found that youngsters who were less proficient at problem-focused coping had more emotional/behavioral problems. A positive relationship was found between emotion-focused coping and emotional/behavioral problems; however, many of the emotion-focused strategies used were maladaptive efforts such as "hit the other person" or "yelled at the other person." Thus, emotion-focused coping did not appear to be well developed in this age group.

Using a somewhat older sample, Wills (1986) studied the relationship between stress, coping, and substance use in twelve- to fifteen-year-olds (seventh and eighth graders). Results indicated that stress was positively related to substance use. In addition, both behavioral coping (problem focused) and cognitive coping and relaxation (emotion focused) were inversely related to substance use, particularly when high stress levels were present. Thus, these coping strategies seemed to buffer the effects of stress.

Coping skills are sets of information and learned physiological, social, cognitive, and/or affective behaviors that individuals purposefully use to deal effectively with stressors and to decrease negative stress reactions. Coping skills allow individuals to respond constructively to potentially stressful situations by executing a specific set of actions. Since coping skills consist of information and learned behaviors, they can be taught as a way to increase the effectiveness with which individuals appraise and respond to potential stressors. Coping skills directly improve our ability to deal with specific stressors; they also increase our tendency to see ourselves as capable of meeting constructively the demands of a variety of potentially threatening situations.

### Summary

Stress can be best defined as a process involving a potential stressor, an individual's characteristics, and that person's stress reaction. A variety of stressors have been identified that potentially can have negative effects on child and adolescent mental health, physical health, and social adjustment. These negative effects can be reduced through environmental manipulations that would eliminate stressors; however, given the nature of many stressors this would be difficult, if not impossible. Children and adolescents can reduce or eliminate many of their problems related to stressors by learning and using coping skills.

Coping skills can be employed by the individual to mediate the effects of potential stressors and to deal with them constructively. Coping skills are sets of learned, purposeful, individual responses to stressors that increase positive outcomes in stressful situations and reduce or eliminate negative stressful states. Recent studies have found that children and adolescents use coping behaviors in response to stressors, and that those who are less proficient at coping have more emotional/behavioral problems. Subsequent chapters in this book will describe and examine a range of coping skills interventions that can be implemented with children and adolescents in school settings. The goal of these interventions is to teach children and adolescents personal and social coping skills that can assist them in dealing with potential stressors they encounter in their daily lives and the stress reactions that may result from these situations.

# Two

# Learning to Relax

The ability to relax is a coping skill that can help children and adolescents control their physiological responses in potentially stressful situations; it can also help them reduce their anxiety response to stressors or other types of physiological overarousal once it occurs. Over the past fifteen years, relaxation training has become an increasingly popular means of helping youngsters develop this skill.

## Development

Relaxation training procedures were originally developed for use with adults (Jacobson, 1938), most often in conjunction with systematic desensitization (Wolpe, 1962), a psychotherapeutic procedure typically used to reduce fear or anxiety. Systematic desensitization is based on the idea that an anxiety response can be inhibited by substituting a response that is incompatible with anxiety. This incompatible response is relaxation or calmness. Systematic desensitization is conducted in three stages: (1) training in deep muscle relaxation; (2) construction of a smoothly graded hierarchy of anxiety-provoking scenes; and (3) systematic desensitization proper, in which the client imagines scenes from the anxiety hierarchy counterposed with the experience of relaxation. Systematic desensitization has become the most frequently used behavior therapy procedure for dealing with children's fears and phobias (Ollendick, 1979).

Subsequent to the development and evaluation of systematic desensitization, therapists began using relaxation training procedures to teach children and adolescents how to cope actively with anxiety and a variety of other problems that may result from stressful situations. The literature reports some use of a procedure with children that is called self-control desensitization (Bornstein & Knapp, 1981; DiNardo & DiNardo, 1981). This approach conceptualizes desensitization as a way to train the child to cope with anxiety. After being trained in relaxation, the child is told to apply it whenever he or she feels anxiety or tension. In addition, during desensitization, the child is encouraged to practice imagining anxiety-producing scenes and relaxing away the anxiety outside of therapy sessions. He or she may also be told to imagine becoming anxious and then coping successfully with the anxiety.

A number of studies have reported the use of relaxation training by itself to treat a variety of children's school-based problems caused by internal and external stressors. These problems include hyperactivity (Braud, 1978; Brown, 1977; Klein & Deffenbacher, 1977; McBrien, 1978; Putre, Loffio, Chorost, Marx, & Gilbert, 1977), generalized anxiety in school (Forman & O'Malley, 1984; Gumaer & Voorneveld, 1975; Kochendofer & Culp, 1979; Meisels, 1976; Rossman & Kahnweiler, 1977), test anxiety (Grant, 1980; Little & Jackson, 1974; Schuchman, 1977), behavior problems (Bergland & Chal, 1972; Elitzer, 1976; Lupin, Braud, Braud, & Duer, 1976; Vacc & Greenleaf, 1980; Wright, 1978), impulsivity and distractibility (Zieffle & Romney, 1985), low reading level (Padawer, 1977), poor handwriting (Carter & Synolds, 1974; Jackson & Hughes, 1978; Jackson, Jolly, & Hamilton, 1980), poor language skills (Bruno-Golden, 1978), poor memory (Barnes, 1976), and negative attitudes toward school (Mead, 1976).

## Procedures

A variety of methods have been used to induce relaxation in children. In the school setting the most often used and appropriate methods are deep muscle relaxation, imagery-based procedures, and deep breathing. These can be used alone or in combination with each other.

### Deep Muscle Relaxation

Deep muscle relaxation training typically involves a series of tension-release cycles performed on various muscle groups. A number of muscle relaxation sequences have been developed for use with children; all follow the same basic format. For a particular muscle group the child is directed to (1) tense the muscle(s), (2) hold the tension for a few seconds while focusing on the tense feelings, (3) relax the muscle(s), and (4) notice the difference between the feelings of tension and relaxation and focus on the pleasant feelings of relaxation for a few seconds.

Morris and Kratochwill (1983, pp. 135–136) present a muscle relaxation sequence that is a modified version of the technique developed by Jacobson (1938). The procedure typically requires twenty to twenty-five minutes; each step takes about ten seconds with a ten- to fifteen-second pause between steps. The steps, as they should be presented by the trainer, are as follows:

1.  Take a deep breath and hold it (for about 10 seconds). Hold it. Okay, let it out.
2.  Raise both of your hands about half way above the couch (or arms of the chair) and breathe normally. Now, drop your hands to the couch (or down).
3.  Now hold your arms out and make a tight fist. Really tight. Feel the tension in your hands. I am going to count to three and when I say "three" I

*Source:* From Richard J. Morris and Thomas R. Kratochwill, *Teaching Children's Fears and Phobias: A Behavioral Approach.* Copyright © 1983. Reprinted with permission of Allyn and Bacon. Appeared originally in "Fear reduction methods" by Morris, in *Helping People Change,* edited by F. H. Kanfer and A. P. Goldstein. Copyright © 1980 by Pergamon Press.

want you to drop your hands. One . . . Two
. . . Three.

4. Raise your arms again, and bend your fingers back
the other way (toward your body). Now drop your
hands and relax.

5. Raise your arms. Now drop them and relax.

6. Now raise your arms again, but this time "flap"
your hands around. Okay, relax again.

7. Raise your arms again. Now relax.

8. Raise your arms above the couch (chair) again and
tense your biceps until they shake. Breathe normally,
and keep your hands loose. Relax your hands. (Notice how you have a warm feeling of relaxation.)

9. Now hold your arms out to your side and tense
your biceps. Make sure that you breathe normally.
Relax your arms.

10. Now arch your shoulders back. Hold it. Make sure
that your arms are relaxed. Now relax.

11. Hunch your shoulders back. Hold it. Make sure
that your arms are relaxed. Now relax.

12. Now turn your head to the right and tense your
neck. Relax and bring your head back again to its
natural position.

13. Turn your head to the left and tense your neck.
Relax and bring your head back again to its natural
position.

14. Now bend your head back slightly toward the
chair. Hold it. Okay, now bring your head back
slowly to its natural position.

15. This time bring your head down almost to your
chest. Hold it. Now relax and let your head come
back to its natural resting position.

16. Now, open your mouth as much as possible. A little wider, okay, relax. (Mouth must be partly open
at end.)

17. Now tense your lips by closing your mouth. Okay,
relax.

18. Put your tongue at the roof of your mouth. Press

hard, (pause) relax and allow your tongue to come to a comfortable position in your mouth.

19. Now put your tongue at the bottom of your mouth. Press down hard. Relax and let your tongue come to a comfortable position in your mouth.

20. Now just lie (sit) there and relax. Try not to think of anything.

21. To control self-verbalization, I want you to go through the motions of singing a high note—not aloud! Okay, start singing to yourself. Hold that note. Now relax. (You are becoming more and more relaxed.)

22. Now sing a medium tone and make your vocal cords tense again. Relax.

23. Now sing a medium tone and make your vocal cords tense again. Relax. (Your vocal apparatus should be relaxed now. Relax your mouth.)

24. Now close your eyes. Squeeze them tight and breathe naturally. Notice the tension. Now relax. (Notice how the pain goes away when you relax.)

25. Now let your eyes relax and keep your mouth open slightly.

26. Open your eyes as much as possible. Hold it. Now relax your eyes.

27. Now wrinkle your forehead as much as possible. Hold it. Okay, relax.

28. Now take a deep breath and hold it. Relax.

29. Now exhale. Breathe all the air out . . . all of it out. Relax. (Notice the wondrous feeling of breathing again.)

30. Imagine that there are weights pulling on all your muscles making them flaccid and relaxed . . . pulling your arms and body into the couch.

31. Pull your stomach muscles together. Tighter. Okay, relax.

32. Now extend your muscles as if you were a prize fighter. Make your stomach hard. Relax. (You are becoming more and more relaxed.)

33. Now tense your buttocks. Tighter. Hold it. Now relax.

34. Now search the upper part of your body and relax any part that is tense. First the facial muscles. (Pause 3–5 seconds.) Then the vocal muscles. (Pause 3–5 seconds.) The neck region. (Pause 3–5 seconds.) Your shoulders . . . relax any part which is tense. (Pause) Now the arms and fingers. Relax these. Becoming very relaxed.

35. Maintaining this relaxation, raise both of your legs (about a 45-degree angle). Now relax. (Notice that this further relaxes you.)

36. Now bend your feet back so that your toes point toward your face. Relax your mouth. Bend them hard. Relax.

37. Bend your feet the other way . . . away from your body. Not far. Notice the tension. Okay, relax.

38. Relax. (Pause) Now curl your toes together as hard as you can. Tighter. Okay, relax. (Quiet . . . silence for about 30 seconds.)

39. This completes the formal relaxation procedure. Now explore your body from your feet up. Make sure that every muscle is relaxed. (Say slowly) First your toes, your feet, your legs, buttocks, stomach, shoulder, neck, eyes, and finally your forehead—all should be relaxed now. (Quiet—silence for about 10 seconds.) Just lie there and feel very relaxed, noticing the warmness of the relaxation. (Pause) I would like you to stay this way for about one more minute, and then I am going to count to five. When I reach five, I want you to open your eyes feeling very calm and refreshed. (Quiet—silence for about one minute.) Okay, when I count to five I want you to open your eyes feeling very calm and refreshed. One . . . feeling very calm; two . . . very calm, very refreshed; three . . . very refreshed; four . . . and five.

Morris and Kratochwill (1983) indicate that most children become somewhat proficient at relaxation after three training sessions. At this point, the trainer should encourage the child to practice the relaxation method at home. These practice sessions should last ten to fifteen minutes and take place at least twice a day. The child can be given a cassette tape of the procedure to facilitate practice.

Cautela and Groden (1978) have developed a relaxation training manual with deep muscle relaxation procedures designed specifically for use with children. Sets of instructions are provided in the manual for children over eight years old as well as younger children or children with special needs. The manual also contains illustrations for each step in the relaxation sequence and simple verbal descriptions of each step.

The instructions for children over eight contain tension-relaxation cycles for fourteen muscle groups in which muscles are tensed for five seconds and relaxed for ten seconds. In addition, breathing procedures and procedures for practicing relaxing in a variety of body positions (while standing, walking, and lying down) are presented. An example of the written instructions of one muscle group is as follows.

"Put your right arm out straight, make a fist, and tighten your whole arm from your hand to your shoulder. Notice where it feels tense (biceps, forearm, back of arm, elbow, above and below wrist and fingers). Pay special attention to those areas that are particularly tense. Gradually relax and lower your arm, bending it at the elbow; relax so that your arm is resting on your lap in the relaxing position. Notice how it feels to have those muscles loosen, switch off, relax, and the difference in the way they feel. Repeat with the left arm" (Cautela & Groden, 1978, p. 28).

The procedures for children under eight and children with special needs are modifications of the procedures for older children. Only gross motor areas including arms, hands, and legs are addressed. The relaxation sequence for each muscle group is similar to the sequence for older children in that it involves (1) tensing the muscles to a maximum degree, (2) noticing the feelings of tension for about two seconds, (3) relaxing the muscles, and (4) enjoying the feeling of relaxation for about ten seconds.

Cautela and Groden (1978) point out that certain prerequisite skills are necessary before relaxation training is appropriate; they include a relaxation readiness pretest in their manual. If the child successfully performs the pretest behaviors, then relaxation training can proceed. If a particular behavior is not in the child's repertoire, that skill must be trained before relaxation is initiated. They further indicate that in teaching very young children relaxation readiness and/or relaxation skills, concrete reinforcers may be needed. In addition, it may be necessary to guide the child through the movements physically at first, or to use special apparatus, such as squeeze toys, to facilitate appropriate movement. The relaxation readiness pretest of Cautela and Groden (1978, p. 41) is presented below.

### Phase I. Basic Skills

1. Ask the child to sit quietly in a chair for 5 seconds, feet still, back straight, head up, without moving or vocalizing. Repeat 2 more times.
2. Say "Look at me," and ask the child to maintain eye contact for 3 seconds. Child must respond within 5 seconds. Repeat 2 more times.

### Phase II. Imitative Skills

3. Say "Do this," and raise your hand above your head. Child should imitate this response correctly within 5 seconds. Repeat 2 more times.
4. Say "Do this," and you tap the table. Child should be able to imitate this response correctly by tapping the table. Repeat 2 more times.
5. Say "Do this," and tap your chest. Child should be able to imitate correctly by tapping his chest. Repeat 2 more times.

*Phase III. Following Simple Instructions*

6.  Say "Stand up." Child should stand up in front of his chair within 5 seconds. Repeat this instruction 2 more times.
7.  Say "Sit down." Child should sit down in his chair within 5 seconds. Repeat this instruction 2 more times.
8.  Stand 6 feet from the child and say "Come here." Child should stand up and walk toward you without inappropriate movements or vocalizations. Repeat 2 more times.

Ollendick and Cerny (1981, pp. 70–72) have also developed a deep muscle relaxation script for use with children. They recommend use of fifteen- to twenty-minute training sessions twice a week during which about three muscle groups are introduced per session. Their script is as follows.

### Head and Arms

Make a fist with your left hand. Squeeze it hard. Feel the tightness in your hand and arm as your squeeze. Now let your hand go and relax. See how much better your hand and arm feel when they are relaxed. Once again, make a fist with your left hand and squeeze hard. Good. Now relax and let your hand go. (Repeat the process—the right hand and arm.)

### Arms and Shoulders

Stretch your arms out in front of you. Raise them high up over your head. Way back. Feel the pull in your shoulders. Stretch higher. Now just let your arms drop back to your side. Okay, let's stretch again. Stretch your arms out in front of you. Raise them over your head. Pull

*Note:* The relaxation training script excerpted here is from Ollendick, T. H., & Cerny, J. (1981). *Clinical behavior therapy with children.* New York: Plenum Press.

them back, way back. Pull hard. Now let them drop quickly. Good. Notice how your shoulders feel more relaxed. This time let's have a great big stretch. Try to touch the ceiling. Stretch your arms way out in front of you. Raise them way up high over your head. Push them way back. Notice the tension and pull in your arms and shoulders. Hold tight now. Great. Let them drop very quickly and feel how good it is to be relaxed. It feels good and warm and lazy.

### Shoulder and Neck

Try to pull your shoulders up to yours ears and push your head down into your shoulders. Hold it tight. Okay, now relax and feel the warmth. Again, pull your shoulders up to your ears and push your head down into your shoulders. Do it tightly. Okay, you can relax now. Bring your head out and let your shoulders relax. Notice how much better it feels to be relaxed than to be all tight. One more time now. Push your head down and your shoulders way up to your ears. Hold it. Feel the tenseness in your neck and shoulders. Okay. You can relax now and feel comfortable. You feel good.

### Jaw

Put your teeth together real hard. Let your neck muscles help you. Now relax. Just let your jaw hang loose. Notice how good it feels just to let your jaw drop. Okay, bite down again hard. That's good. Now relax again. Just let your jaw drop. It feels so good just to let go. Okay, one more time. Bite down. Hard as you can. Harder. Oh, you're really working hard. Good. Now relax. Try to relax your whole body. Let yourself go as loose as you can.

### Face and Nose

Wrinkle up your nose. Make as many wrinkles in your nose as you can. Scrunch your nose up real hard. Good.

Now you can relax your nose. Now wrinkle up your nose again. Wrinkle it up hard. Hold it just as tight as you can. Okay. You can relax your face. Notice that when you scrunch up your nose that your cheeks and your mouth and your forehead all help you and they get tight, too. So when you relax your nose, your whole face is relaxed too, and that feels good. Now make lots of wrinkles on your forehead. Hold it tight, now. Okay, you can let go. Now you can just relax. Let your face go smooth. No wrinkles anywhere. Your face feels nice and smooth and relaxed.

### Stomach

Now tighten up your stomach muscles real tight. Make your stomach real hard. Don't move. You can relax now. Let your stomach go soft. Let it be as relaxed as you can. That feels so much better. Okay, again, tighten your stomach real hard. Good. You can relax now. Kind of settle down, get comfortable, and relax. Notice the difference between a tight stomach and a relaxed one. That's how we want to feel. Nice and loose and relaxed. Okay. Once more. Tighten up. Tighten hard. Good. Now you can relax completely. You can feel nice and relaxed.

This time, try to pull your stomach in. Try to squeeze it against your back bone. Try to be as skinny as you can. Now relax. You don't have to be skinny now. Just relax and feel your stomach being warm and loose. Okay, squeeze in your stomach again. Make it touch your backbone. Get it real small and tight. Get as skinny as you can. Hold tight now. You can relax now. Settle back and let your stomach come back out where it belongs. You can really feel good now. You've done fine.

### Legs and Feet

Push your toes down on the floor real hard. You'll probably need your legs to help you push. Push down, spread your toes apart. Now relax your feet. Let your toes go loose and feel how nice that is. It feels good to be relaxed. Okay. Now push your toes down. Let your leg muscles help you push your feet down. Push your feet. Hard. Okay. Relax your feet, relax your legs, relax your toes. It feels so good to be relaxed. No tenseness anywhere. You feel kind of warm and tingly.

## Conclusion

Stay as relaxed as you can. Let your whole body go limp and feel all your muscles relaxed. In a few minutes I will ask you to open your eyes and that will be the end of the session. Today is a good day, and you are ready to go back to class feeling very relaxed. You've worked hard in here and it feels good to work hard. Shake your arms. Now shake your legs. Move your head around. Slowly open your eyes. Very good. You've done a good job. You're going to be a super relaxer.

The goal of each of these relaxation training procedures is to teach children methods of relaxing in day-to-day situations during which they may notice themselves becoming tense or anxious. Thus, relaxation can be used as a coping skill. In order to make the transition from practicing the tension-release sequences to using relaxation as a coping skill on a daily basis, fading procedures must be employed. Typically a cue word such as "relax" or "switch-off" is incorporated in the instructions for each muscle group. After tension-release cycles are practiced a number of times, the child is instructed to practice relaxing each muscle group in the sequence without first tensing. Next, the relaxation sequence is shortened by having the child address larger muscle groups. Finally, the child should be able to relax his or her entire body by thinking a cue word (such as "relax").

*Imagery.* Imagery procedures have also been used to help children achieve a relaxed state. Imagery is thought to be especially helpful for children because it attracts and maintains interest. Kendall and Braswell (1985) suggest a game called "Robot–Rag Doll" during which trainer and child first act like robots (stiff and tense and walking without bending limbs) and then like rag dolls (floppy, relaxed, limp). Koeppen (1974, pp. 17–20) developed the following relaxation training script based on imagery.

### Hands and Arms

Pretend you have a whole lemon in your left hand. Now squeeze it hard. Try to squeeze all the juice out. Feel the tightness in your hand and arm as you squeeze. Now drop the lemon. Notice how your muscles feel when they are relaxed. Take another lemon and squeeze it. Try to squeeze this one harder than you did the first one. That's right. Real hard. Now drop your lemon and relax. See how much better your hand and arm feel when they are relaxed. Once again, take a lemon in your left hand and squeeze all the juice out. Don't leave a single drop. Squeeze hard. Good. Now relax and let the lemon fall from your hand. (Repeat the process for the right hand and arm.)

### Arms and Shoulders

Pretend you are a furry, lazy cat. You want to stretch. Stretch your arms out in front of you. Raise them up high over your head. Way back. Feel the pull in your shoulders. Stretch higher. Now just let your arms drop back to your side. Okay, kitten, stretch again. Stretch your arms out in front of you. Raise them over your head. Pull them back, way back. Pull hard. Now let them drop quickly. Good. Notice how your shoulders feel more relaxed. This time let's have a great big stretch. Try to touch the ceiling. Stretch your arms way out in front of you. Raise them way up high over your head. Push them way, way back. Notice the tension and pull in your arms and shoulders. Hold tight, now. Great. Let them

*Note:* The relaxation training script based on imagery is reprinted from Koeppen, A. S. (1974). Relaxation training for children. *Elementary School Guidance and Counseling, 9,* 17–20. © AACD. Reprinted with permission. No further reproduction authorized without written permission of American Association for Counseling and Development.

drop very quickly and feel how good it is to be relaxed. It feels good and warm and lazy.

### Shoulders and Neck

Now pretend you are a turtle. You're sitting out on a rock by a nice, peaceful pond, just relaxing in the warm sun. It feels nice and warm and safe here. Oh-Oh! You sense danger. Pull your head into your house. Try to pull in your shoulders. It isn't easy to be a turtle in a shell. The danger is past now. You can come into the warm sunshine and once again, you can relax and feel the warm sunshine. Watch out now! More danger. Hurry, pull your head back into your house and hold it tight. You have to be closed in tight to protect yourself. Okay, you can relax now. Bring your head out and let your shoulders relax. Notice how much better it feels to be relaxed than to be all tight. One more time, now. Danger! Pull your head in. Push your shoulders way up to your ears and hold tight. Don't let even a tiny piece of your head show outside your shell. Hold it. Feel the tenseness in your neck and shoulders. Okay. You can come out now. It's safe again. Relax and feel comfortable in your safety. There's no more danger. Nothing to worry about. Nothing to be afraid of. You feel good.

### Jaw

You have a giant jawbreaker bubble gum in your mouth. It's very hard to chew. Bite down on it. Hard! Let your neck muscles help you. Now relax. Just let your jaw hang loose. Notice how good it feels just to let your jaw drop. Okay, let's tackle that jawbreaker again now. Bite down. Hard! Try to squeeze it out between your teeth. That's good. You're really tearing that gum up. Now relax again. Just let your jaw drop off your face. It feels so good just to let go and not have to fight that bubble gum. Okay, one more time. We're really going to tear it up this time. Bite down. Hard as you can. Harder. Oh, you're really working hard. Good. Now relax. Try to relax your whole body. You've beaten the bubble gum. Let yourself go as loose as you can.

### Face and Nose

Here comes a pesky old fly. He has landed on your nose. Try to get him off without using your hands. That's right, wrinkle up your nose. Make as many wrinkles in your nose as you can. Scrunch your nose up real hard. Good. You've chased him away. Now you can relax your nose. Oops, here he comes back again. Shoo him off. Wrinkle it up hard. Hold it up hard. Hold it just as tight as you can. Okay he flew away. You can relax your face. Notice that when you scrunch up your nose that your cheeks and your mouth and your forehead and your eyes all help you, and they get tight too. So when you relax your nose, your whole face relaxes too, and that feels good. Oh-oh. This time that old fly has come back, but this time he's on your forehead. Make lots of wrinkles. Try to catch him between all those wrinkles. Hold it tight, now. Okay, you can let go. He's gone for good. Now you can just relax. Let your face go smooth, no wrinkles anywhere. Your face feels nice and smooth and relaxed.

### Stomach

Hey! Here comes a cute baby elephant. But he's not watching where he's going. He doesn't see you lying there in the grass, and he's about to step on your stomach. Don't move. You don't have time to get out of the way. Just get ready for him. Make your stomach very hard. Tighten up your stomach muscles real tight. Hold it. It looks like he is going the other way. You can relax now. Let your stomach go soft. Let it be as relaxed as you can. That feels so much better. Oops, he's this way again. Get ready. Tighten up your stomach. Real hard. If he steps on you when your stomach is hard, it won't hurt. Make your stomach into a rock. Okay, he's moving away again. You can relax now. Kind of settle down, get comfortable, and relax. Notice the difference between a tight stomach and a relaxed one. That's how we want it to feel—nice and loose and relaxed. You won't believe this, but this time he's really coming your way and not turning around. He's headed straight for you. Tighten up. Tighten hard. Here he comes. This is really it. You've got to hold on tight. He's stepping on you. He's stepped over you. Now he's gone for good. You can relax completely. You're safe. Everything is okay, and you can feel nice and relaxed.

This time imagine that you want to squeeze through a narrow fence and the boards have splinters on them. You'll have to make yourself very skinny if you're going to make it through. Suck your stomach in. Try to squeeze it up against your backbone. Try to be as skinny as you can. You've got to get through. Now relax. You don't have to be skinny now, just relax and feel your stomach being warm and loose. Okay, let's try to get through that fence now. Squeeze up your stomach. Make it touch your backbone. Get it real small and tight. Get as skinny as you can. Hold tight now. You've got to squeeze through. You got through that skinny little fence and no splinters. You can relax now. Settle back and let your stomach come back out where it belongs. You can feel really good now. You've done fine.

### Legs and Feet

Now pretend that you are standing barefoot in a big, fat mud puddle. Squish your toes down deep into the mud. Try to get your feet down to the bottom of the mud puddle. You'll probably need your legs to help you push. Push down, spread your toes apart, and feel the mud squish up between your toes. Now step out of the mud puddle. Relax your feet. Let your toes go loose and feel how nice that is. It feels good to be relaxed. Back into the mud puddle. Squish your toes down. Let your leg muscles help you push your feet down. Push your feet. Hard. Try to squeeze that mud puddle dry. Okay. Come back

out now. Relax your feet, relax your legs, relax your toes.
It feels so good to be relaxed. No tenseness anywhere.
You feel kind of warm and tingly.

Ollendick and Cerny (1981) reported two studies that evaluated their muscle relaxation script as well as Koeppen's (1974) script. They found that following three 15-minute training sessions, both procedures resulted in significantly reduced muscle tension levels for normal six- and seven-year-olds while a control condition had no effect. In addition, both procedures reduced muscle tension for hyperactive and aggressive six-, seven-, and eight-year-olds, although the Ollendick and Cerny procedure produced greater reductions.

Robin, Schneider, and Dolnick (1976) reported on a self-control relaxation program called the turtle technique that emphasized imagery. The purpose of this program was to help emotionally disturbed children control their aggressive behavior. The image of a turtle was used to teach the children to react to aggressive impulses by (1) imagining that they were turtles withdrawing into their shells, putting their arms close to their bodies, putting their heads down, and closing their eyes; (2) relaxing their muscles to cope with tension; and (3) using social problem solving to generate prosocial alternative behaviors. Regular classroom teachers implemented the program under the guidance of psychologist consultants, and results indicated significant decreases in aggressive classroom behavior.

Relaxation can also be induced by having children imagine elaborate relaxing real-world images (Kendall & Braswell, 1985), such as lying on the beach or sitting in front of a fireplace. Success imagery is an additional relaxation procedure in which the child imagines feeling calm and doing well in a potentially stressful situation (Gerler & Danielson, 1984).

After reviewing relevant research, Jay, Ozolins, Elliott, and Caldwell (1983) concluded that seven- and eight-year-old children were able to produce and manipulate images. Thus, imagery would be appropriate for use with children seven years old and over. Wielkiewicz (1986) states that imagery is most effective when its content is at least partially determined by the child. He suggests having children draw a picture of themselves doing something relaxing and using the child's picture as the basis for a relaxing image.

## Deep Breathing

A final procedure used to help children and adolescents relax themselves is deep breathing. At times deep breathing is trained in isolation, although most often it is used in conjunction with deep muscle relaxation. The procedure generally calls for the child to take a deep breath, hold it, and then exhale slowly. While exhaling, he or she tries to relax the whole body from head to toe. In addition, as the child exhales, he or she concentrates on a cue word such as "relax" or "one." Cautela and Groden (1978) indicate that toys such as whistles, harmonicas, party horns, pinwheels, and bubble wands can be used to teach young children the initial behaviors necessary for deep breathing.

### Review of Research

In a review of studies of relaxation training for school-based problems, Richter (1984) concluded that positive results could be achieved if specific treatment conditions were provided. These include extending the length of training to at least six weeks and providing environmental supports in the form of parent and/or teacher involvement and training. Specific school behaviors such as reading and language acquisition appear to be responsive to relaxation training when the child's performance is initially significantly below average and the below-average performance is related to tension and anxiety. However, this review indicated that relaxation is not an effective treatment for serious, long-standing behavioral disorders if it is used in isolation to the exclusion of other treatment procedures.

Recent studies have extended the range of problems for which school-based relaxation training can be used successfully. Reynolds and Coats (1986) investigated the effectiveness of cognitive-behavioral therapy and relaxation training for the treatment of depression in adolescents. They examined the use of relaxation training because previous studies with adults had indicated that relaxation could effectively reduce the symptoms of depression, research evidence has linked stress with depression, and relaxation has been conceptualized as a coping strategy that can help the individual deal with stress.

The subjects in their study met in small groups for ten 50-minute sessions over five weeks in a high school setting. Therapy was conducted by a school psychologist. The training emphasized the relationship between stress, muscle tension, and depression. Deep muscle relaxation training was implemented and subjects were taught to use relaxation skills in situations noted for producing tension. Both the cognitive-behavioral and relaxation training groups were superior to a wait-list control group in the reduction of depressive symptoms at posttest and five-week follow-up assessments.

Ewart and others (1987) reported on a successful innovative school-based health promotion program that utilized relaxation training as a means of reducing cardiovascular risk. Fourteen hundred students in grades 9 and 10 at two large urban public high schools underwent blood pressure screening. Those with blood pressure above the eighty-fifth percentile were randomly assigned to either a twelve-week progressive muscle relaxation training program given as part of a health education elective class or a control condition.

The relaxation intervention included training in four skills: (1) assuming a relaxed posture, (2) muscle relaxation, (3) slow diaphragmatic breathing, and (4) handwarming. Behavioral goals were established for each of the four skills and students were given feedback on their progress. Students were encouraged to experiment with different relaxation methods to find one that was most helpful for them. About fifteen to twenty minutes of relaxation training was provided four days a week for the twelve-week semester. The course was taught by a health education teacher assisted by a master's-level school psychologist.

After presenting five sessions on the cardiovascular system and stress, the health education teacher introduced relaxation. An instructional script guided students in tensing and relaxing muscle groups. The script was rehearsed thirty minutes a day for six days. While the teacher read the script, the school psychologist moved among the students, who were lying on mats, to provide feedback. An abbreviated script was subsequently introduced to encourage students to mentally scan their bodies for tension and to relax. Exercises in deep breathing, mental imagery, and handwarming were then introduced. Beginning at the seventh week, relaxation sessions were conducted with students sitting at their desks to encourage generalization. Students were given relaxation tapes and told to practice daily at home.

Results indicated that treatment students enjoyed the sessions, mastered the technique, and achieved reduced systolic blood pressure at posttest relative to untrained controls. However, at four-month follow-up, group differences were not significant, indicating the importance of continuous incorporation of relaxation training in the school routine. This study indicated the potential of school-based relaxation training as a health promotion technique.

## Summary

Relaxation training can provide an effective set of coping skills for children and adolescents faced with stressors that typically produce anxiety and tension as stress reactions. Muscle relaxation, relaxation through imagery, and deep breathing are three approaches to relaxation training that can be used separately or in combination. These procedures have been used effectively in both treatment and prevention programs with children from early elementary school through high school. They have been implemented successfully by classroom teachers, who have received special training, as well as special services providers. Studies appear to indicate that environmental support, in the form of teacher and parent involvement, may be necessary to ensure practice outside of training sessions and continued use of relaxation skills after initial training has terminated. Such practice is needed to maximize the effectiveness of these procedures.

# Three

# Facilitating
# Social Problem Solving

Social problem-solving approaches to developing coping skills in children and adolescents focus on teaching a systematic means of dealing with social problem situations through a structured sequence of cognitive activity. Social problem solving has been defined as a component of social competence consisting of a set of skills used to resolve social conflicts (Gesten & Weissberg, 1986). In the relatively early stages of research on and development of social problem solving, Spivack and Shure (1974), two of the major proponents of this approach, stated that children's adjustment could be improved if "one can enhance their ability to see a human problem, their appreciation of different ways of handling it, and their sensitivity to the potential consequences of what they do" (p. 21).

## Development

Most of the research related to the social problem-solving approach has been conducted since 1970. However, in 1942, Chittenden provided a very early example of a training program designed to help

children deal better with social situations by increasing cooperative-
ness and decreasing attempts at domination. The training program
had three objectives: to teach the child (1) to identify potential problem play situations involving disagreements with others, (2) to find
ways to work out disagreements such as by taking turns and sharing, and (3) to use appropriate ways of initiating interaction in this
type of play situation. Although the report provided some positive
results, the approach was not addressed further until many years
later. In 1958, Jahoda suggested that mental health is related to an
individual's ability to solve interpersonal problems. This ability
was hypothesized to consist of a tendency to recognize and admit a
problem, to reflect on possible solutions, to make a decision, and
to take action. In the early 1970s, D'Zurilla and Goldfried elaborated
on use of the social problem-solving approach with adults, and
Spivack and Shure at the Hahnemann Medical College began an
extensive series of studies that explored use of social problem solving with children.

     D'Zurilla and Goldfried (1971) define problem solving as "a
behavioral process, whether overt or cognitive in nature, which a)
makes available a variety of potentially effective response alternatives for dealing with the problematic situation and b) increases the
probability of selecting the most effective response from among
these various alternatives" (p. 108). They outlined the problem-
solving process as consisting of five steps: (1) general orientation—
the assumption that problem situations are a normal part of life and
that one can cope with such situations; (2) problem definition and
formulation—definition of the problem in concrete terms; (3) gener-
ation of alternatives—brainstorming all possible solutions; (4) decision making—evaluating each alternative in terms of its likelihood
of solving the problem; and (5) verification—acting on the decision
and evaluating the extent to which the decision was a good one.

     In their work exploring the use of social problem solving to
improve adjustment of children, Spivack, Shure, and their colleagues at the Hahnemann Medical College concentrated on three
major skills: alternative thinking, consequential thinking, and
means-end thinking. Their training programs taught children to
generate multiple solutions to a problem situation, to evaluate the
short-term and long-term consequences of each alternative in mak-

ing a decision, and to plan a series of specific behavioral actions needed to reach a goal.

## Procedures

Social problem-solving training, sometimes called interpersonal problem solving or interpersonal cognitive problem solving (ICPS), emphasizes thinking processes rather than specific cognitive content. The training focuses on teaching the child how to think instead of what to think. Because thinking processes as opposed to thinking content are emphasized, most proponents believe that after training children will be able to apply the strategies they have learned to a wide range of problem situations. Although the individual processes have varied somewhat with particular training programs and research studies, most social problem-solving programs include six major problem-solving steps: (1) identifying the problem, (2) determining goals, (3) generating alternative solutions, (4) examining consequences, (5) choosing the solution, and (6) evaluating the outcome. The child is taught to use the thought processes involved in this problem-solving sequence to change his or her behavior and thereby to resolve social and/or emotional problems. The problem-solving sequence is taught by addressing specific problem situations that the child is dealing with. The same problem-solving steps are repeated in dealing with each problem, providing a problem-solving set for the child to use in dealing with future problems.

The problem identification component of social problem solving focuses on helping the child understand the problem from his or her perspective as well as that of others. The trainer helps the child identify the relevant emotional, social, and environmental aspects of the problem situation. Cartledge and Milburn (1980) suggest using a series of questions to do this. These focus on identifying feelings of being upset, identifying when the upset feelings started, identifying other people present and what their behavior was when the feelings started, and identifying the child's own behavior prior to the onset of upset feelings. Lorion and Work (1987) suggest that through use of role-playing and switching roles, children can learn to view problems from different perspectives.

The second step in solving a social problem involves determining goals. The child is asked to specify a desirable outcome by deciding what he or she would like to have happen instead of what did happen. Lorion and Work (1987) suggest asking the child, "How do you want things to turn out?" The answer to this question provides direction for further problem solving and behavior change efforts.

The third step, generating alternatives, is typically accomplished through brainstorming. The child is asked to suspend judgment and come up with as many ways as possible to deal with the problem situation. The trainer might ask, "What are all the possible things you could do now?" This is frequently done in written format to accommodate lengthy lists of alternatives.

In the next step, the child is asked to go back through the list of alternatives generated and predict the consequence of each alternative behavior. The trainer asks the child, "If you did that, what would probably happen?" Many of the alternatives may have a number of possible consequences, and for each alternative the child is asked to generate as many consequences as he or she can think of to allow for complete consideration of the problem situation. Both immediate and long-term consequences should be examined in determining the costs and benefits of a given solution.

Choosing the solution actually consists of two main tasks. First, the child must decide which alternative has the most probable benefits and least probable costs in light of the original problem and the stated goals. The trainer might facilitate this by asking these questions: "Given what you said you wanted to have happen, which one of these alternatives would be best for you? Which one would be most likely to help you get what you want and avoid what you don't want?" Next, the child must identify the specific manner in which the chosen solution is to be carried out. What will be said? What will nonverbal behavior be like? What will the setting be? When will it be done? What might the reaction of others be and how will the child deal with these reactions? During training, once the specific behaviors involved in implementing the solution are identified, they should be practiced through role-play before the solution is actually implemented. The trainer might first model the desired behavior and then have the child rehearse behaving in the manner planned.

The final step, evaluation, is conducted after the solution is implemented and the child has carried out the behaviors that were chosen. The main questions to be answered by the child in this phase are, Did I do what I set out to do? Did I accomplish what I said I wanted to accomplish? Am I satisfied with the results? If the answers to these questions are yes, then the solution was implemented effectively and the trainer and child can go on to address other problem situations with the problem-solving steps for further practice. If the answer to the first question is no, then the child may need more help in specifying what needs to be done in order to carry out the solution. Alternatively, the child may be able to specify what needs to be done but may need to participate in additional rehearsal role-play activities before the behaviors that make up the solution can be carried out appropriately. If the answer to either of the next two questions is no, then the trainer and child need to examine the list of alternative solutions and consequences and attempt to find a solution that will be more effective in meeting the child's goals.

The types of situations for which the problem-solving approach can be used are wide ranging. Following is an example of the dialogue that might occur between a trainer and an adolescent student:

*Trainer:*   Last week you told me you were worried about being pressured by some of the other kids to try marijuana. Has anything happened this week that got you worried about this again?

*Student:*   Yeah, Jennifer invited me to a party at her house for tomorrow night. She said her parents won't be home.

*Trainer:*   So the problem for you is . . . ?

*Student:*   I know the kids are gonna be smoking marijuana. They're gonna try to get me to do it too. They're gonna say I'm chicken and a baby if I don't. But I don't think I want to. I've heard so many bad things about it lately that it scares me. What if I do something really stupid and messed up after I smoke? I don't think it's good for me. But I don't know what to do.

*Trainer:* So if you go to this party, other kids will try to get you to smoke and you don't know what to do. What's important to you about how this situation might turn out? How do you want things to be with your friends, and with you and drugs?

*Student:* I want to have friends. I want the kids to like me. But I don't want to wind up acting dumb and out of control and do anything really bad. And I don't want to be pushed into doing anything when I'm not sure.

*Trainer:* So what are all the different possibilities of things you could do about this party invitation?

*Student:* I could tell Jennifer I don't want to go. I could tell her I have to do something else with my family. I could go, and then go ahead and smoke. I can go and just tell them that I don't want any when they offer it to me.

*Trainer:* What would happen as a result of each of those things if you actually did them?

*Student:* If I told Jennifer that I didn't want to go without saying anything else, she would probably get mad at me or feel hurt. If I told her I had to do something else with my family, she'd understand and wouldn't think anything of it. But I might feel a little bad because I wasn't really telling her the truth. If I go to the party and smoke, I might wind up doing things that are bad for me, like get carried away with my boyfriend. I might say things I don't really mean. My parents might notice that I'm acting funny when I get home and then I'd really be in trouble. If I go to the party and say no when they offer me some, they'll probably start in on me, telling me I'm a baby, and I don't think I'd have the strength not to finally give in with all of them on me about it.

*Trainer:* So given that you told me you want the kids to like you, but you don't want to wind up doing anything dumb or be pushed into anything, what do you think is the best thing for you to do?

*Student:* I think I should tell her I have to do something with my family that night. Even though it's not totally true, I think it will work out best for me and it really won't hurt anyone else. If I went and tried to say no I don't think I could really handle the way the other kids would act toward me.

Shure and Spivack (1988) have worked extensively with very young urban poor children and provide a description of a program that can be used with preschool and kindergarten children. The training is implemented by teachers who work with small groups of children for twenty minutes per day over four months. This program addresses training of pre-problem-solving skills as well as problem-solving skills because of the age of the target children. The program is conducted using a combination of didactic instruction, discussion, and games.

The first group of lessons focuses on basic language and thinking skills. Words such as *not, some, all, and, or, same,* and *different* are addressed. The concept of "if . . . then" is also introduced. These words and concepts provide the child with prerequisites for determining what and what not to do, for reasoning in terms of cause and effect, for recognizing that particular solutions may be effective with some but not all people, and for developing a variety of solutions.

The next group of lessons focuses on identification of and sensitivity to the child's own feelings and those of others. Children learn to identify the feelings of others by observing their verbal and nonverbal behavior. They also learn that people have different preferences and may react to the same thing differently. In addition, they should discuss how to influence others' feelings. The words *maybe, might, because, why, before, after, now,* and *later* are presented. These concepts provide further understanding of cause and effect in interpersonal relationships; they also underscore the importance of considering multiple perspectives and multiple solutions when dealing with social problems.

The final set of lessons focuses on training of the major interpersonal problem-solving skills. These include generating alternative solutions, identifying consequences, and pairing a problem with solutions and consequences.

In addition to the formal lessons, the teacher uses "dialoguing" to help the child use the problem-solving skills to deal with daily experiences. Dialoguing is a verbal interaction between the child and the teacher in which the teacher assists the child in solving a social problem by helping to structure the child's thought processes to conform to the problem-solving steps. An example of this type of interaction between a teacher and a young child follows.

*Teacher:*   Michael, you're looking very upset. What's wrong?

*Michael:*   I want to play with the computer and Gregory's there.

*Teacher:*   Well, what are some things you can do about this?

*Michael:*   Nothing.

*Teacher:*   Well, yes. I guess that is one thing you could do—nothing—just keep doing what you're doing now—which is sit at your desk and look mad. What would happen if you did that?

*Michael:*   Nothing.

*Teacher:*   Things probably wouldn't change. So what else could you do?

*Michael:*   I could push him off the chair. I could tell him I want to use it.

*Teacher:*   What would happen if you pushed him off the chair?

*Michael:*   I'd get in trouble and he might hit me.

*Teacher:*   What would happen if you told him you wanted to use it?

*Michael:*   He could let me take my turn.

*Teacher:*   So what do you think you should do?

*Michael:*   Ask him.

*Teacher:*   Show me how you'll do that. You make believe I'm Gregory and you say just what you're gonna say to him.

*Michael:*   Gregory, you've been at the computer a long time and I want a turn now.

*Teacher:*   Good. I think you should try that. I think it's a good solution to try. After you try it we can talk about how it worked.

## Specialized Assessment Instruments

A number of specialized assessment instruments have been developed by researchers who have evaluated the effectiveness of social problem-solving training with children and adolescents. Spivack, Shure, Platt, and their colleagues designed instruments to assess the individual subskills contained in their training programs.

The Preschool Interpersonal Problem Solving (PIPS) test (Spivack & Shure, 1974) measures alternative thinking through the number of different and relevant solutions the child can generate. The items consist of verbally presented stories and accompanying pictures reflecting social problem situations with adults and peers. The Means-Ends Problem Solving (MEPS) test (Platt & Spivack, 1977) assesses the child's ability to generate a plan to reach a social goal. It consists of six stories with a beginning and an end, for which the child provides the steps necessary for goal attainment. The What Happens Next game (Spivack & Shure, 1974) measures consequential thinking. The child is presented with social problems and their solutions and is asked what might happen next. These measures have been found to discriminate between various groups of adjusted and maladjusted children. Although originally developed for preschoolers, a number of researchers have adapted these measures for older children and adolescents (Tisdelle & St. Lawrence, 1986).

More recently, Lochman and Lampron (1986) developed the Problem-Solving Measure for Conflict (PSMC). This instrument contains problems involving interpersonal conflict with parents, teachers, and peers. The quality as well as the quantity of responses is scored. This scale has been found to differentiate aggressive from nonaggressive children.

## Review of Research

A sizable body of research has focused on the use and effectiveness of the social problem-solving approach with children and adolescents. Some studies have examined the role social problem-solving skills play in child and adolescent adjustment; others have investigated the efficacy of social problem-solving training programs as a means of treating identified problems or preventing potential problems.

## Problem-Solving Skills and Adjustment

Although findings have not been entirely consistent, a number of studies have linked child adjustment to skill at alternative thinking and means-end thinking. The ability to generate alternative solutions has been linked to adjustment at a variety of age levels including preschool (Shure & Spivack, 1978, 1980; Spivack & Shure, 1974), kindergarten (Shure & Spivack, 1980), elementary school (Shure, 1980), and adolescence (Platt, Spivack, Altman, Altman, & Peizer, 1974). The ability to generate a series of actions through which a social problem can be solved has been linked to adjustment for elementary school students (Shure & Spivack, 1972) and adolescents (Spivack & Shure, 1974). In a review of the literature in this area, Kendall and Fischler (1984) concluded that alternative thinking skills were related to adjustment during early childhood and middle childhood, and that means-end thinking skills were related to adjustment during middle childhood and adolescence. The roles of other specific subskills in the problem-solving sequence have yet to be substantiated.

## Prevention Studies

The early work of Spivack and Shure (1974) focused on examining the effectiveness of social problem-solving training with children who were at risk for developing serious problems. Inner-city, lower-class, black nursery school children were the subjects of their 1974 study in which the curriculum described in the previous section was implemented. Children who received training made significant gains in alternative and consequential thinking relative to children in a nontreatment control group. In addition, after one year, teachers rated the children in the training group as better adjusted than the control group children. Similar results were also obtained for a group of black inner-city kindergarten children. Teachers implemented the intervention in both of these studies. In a subsequent study Shure and Spivack (1978) trained black, inner-city, lower-class mothers to implement the problem-solving training program with their nursery school children. Compared to control children, children trained by their mothers made increases in alternative and consequential thinking as well as teacher ratings of classroom social behavior.

Sarason and Sarason (1981) examined the effectiveness of social problem-solving training with high school students at risk for delinquency and dropping out of school. After training, students were able to generate more adaptive alternatives to problem situations and were able to make more effective self-presentations in a job interview situation than were control group students. One year later, trained students had fewer absences, less tardiness, and fewer referrals for misbehavior.

In addition to these secondary prevention studies that focus on children at high risk for behavioral and emotional problems, a number of studies have investigated use of social problem solving in a primary prevention context. Primary prevention subjects are normal children with no special propensity toward developing problems other than those present in a normal population. These studies have shown less success and in general appear to indicate gains in cognitive skills without concomitant gains in social behavior (Pellegrini & Urbain, 1985). A notable exception among the relatively early studies is one by Elardo and Caldwell (1979) in which fourth and fifth graders in a middle-class school improved on cognitive measures as well as ratings of social behavior when compared to no-treatment control students.

More recently, Elias and others (1986) used social problem-solving training with fifth graders to help them deal with making the transition from elementary school to middle school. The experimenters felt that negative and inconsistent results of previous studies may have resulted from poor implementation of training curricula. In this study, therefore, psychologists provided extensive training, monitoring, and feedback to the teachers who were implementing the program.

The program lasted through the full academic year and included an instructional phase and an application phase. Three sets of skills were taught: interpersonal sensitivity, means-ends thinking, and planning and anticipation. Interpersonal sensitivity skills included focusing on one's feelings in problem situations, putting those feelings into words, and thinking about one's goal in the situation. Means-end thinking included generating alternative ways to reach one's goal and considering the consequences of these alternatives. Planning and anticipation skills included generating specific ideas for carrying out one's chosen solution, anticipating problems with implementation of that solution, and after using the solution, considering the outcome in planning for future problem situations.

During the instructional phase, problem-solving skills were taught in twenty 40-minute lessons conducted twice a week. Teachers used a curriculum script with the following general format for each lesson: (1) group sharing of occurrences and feelings, (2) brief presentation of the skill to be covered, (3) presentation of a sample situation related to the skill through a story or videotaped vignette, (4) dialoguing-based discussion of the situation and the skill, (5) role-play, and (6) summary and review. During the application phase, teachers used activities to bring problem solving into regular classroom activities; they mediated social conflicts between students by helping them to engage in the problem-solving process. Children receiving this training reported experiencing fewer and less intense stressors in middle school than children receiving partial training or no training.

## Treatment Studies

A number of studies have also been conducted to examine the effectiveness of social problem solving with children or adolescents who have been identified as possessing emotional and/or behavioral problems. Prior to the intervention, nursery school subjects in the 1974 study conducted by Spivack and Shure were identified by their teachers as either well adjusted, impulsive and aggressive, or inhibited. The program was successful for all subjects, as discussed above. The problem-solving approach has also shown positive effects on behavior of primary grade children in special education classes for the emotionally disturbed (Robin, Schneider, & Dolnick, 1976) through reductions in aggressive behavior. In addition, social problem solving has been successful with very seriously maladjusted young people, such as incarcerated juvenile delinquents (Ollendick & Hersen, 1979).

## Summary

The social problem-solving approach to building coping skills has shown success in the prevention and treatment of a variety of social problems of children and adolescents. Social problem-solving training programs typically focus on teaching the use of six problem-solving steps in addressing social problems: (1) identifying the problem, (2) determining goals, (3) generating alternative solutions, (4) examining consequences, (5) choosing the solution, and (6) evaluating the outcome.

In a recent review of social problem-solving training issues, Shure and Spivack (1988) point out that the approach is applicable to a variety of racial, ethnic, and age groups. Social problem-solving training can be conducted by teachers, allowing large numbers of students to be trained in a cost-effective manner. Shure and Spivack (1988) also point out that the program can be implemented without lengthy preparation, as many of the curriculum manuals that have been developed contain specific, easy-to-follow instructions. This statement, however, must be viewed cautiously; the 1986 study by Elias and others, described previously, seems to indicate that the more successful training programs are those in which implementation issues are carefully attended to, and that school personnel may need fairly extensive training and posttraining consultation to implement social problem-solving programs in the classroom appropriately.

Shure and Spivack (1988) also state that for optimal impact, training should last for at least four months. This view is supported by a number of studies that appear to indicate less successful outcomes for short programs than for longer programs in which there is ample time for practice of new skills.

The approach is one that can easily be incorporated into the regular school curriculum. The content is related to a number of academic subjects such as science, language, and social studies, making this approach a particularly appealing one to school administrators and classroom teachers.

# Four

Improving Social Interactions

As indicated in Chapter One, situations involving social interaction are frequently sources of stress for children and adolescents. Social skills training programs can teach children and adolescents specific overt verbal and nonverbal behaviors for use in coping with social situations. There are numerous definitions of the term *social skill* in the literature; however, most focus on the idea that social skills are behaviors that produce positive consequences for the user (Cartedge & Milburn, 1978; Foster & Ritchey, 1979). Gresham and Elliott (1987) define social skills as behaviors that help a child attain important social outcomes such as peer group acceptance, positive judgments by significant others, academic competence, positive self-concept, and good psychological adjustment. Combs and Slaby (1978) provide a definition that focuses on both parties involved in an interpersonal relationship by defining social skills as "the ability to interact with others in a given social context in specific ways that are socially acceptable or valued and at the same time personally beneficial, mutually beneficial, or beneficial primarily to others" (p. 162).

Michelson, Sugai, Wood, and Kazdin (1983, p. 3) have identified seven major characteristics of social skills:

"1. Social skills are primarily acquired through learning (e.g.,
    observation, modeling, rehearsal, and feedback).
 2. Social skills comprise specific and discrete verbal and nonver-
    bal behaviors.
 3. Social skills entail both effective and appropriate initiations
    and responses.
 4. Social skills maximize social reinforcement.
 5. Social skills are interactive by nature and entail effective and
    appropriate responsiveness.
 6. Social skill performance is influenced by the characteristics of
    an environment.
 7. Deficits and excesses in social performance can be specified
    and targeted for intervention."

Social skills training remediates deficiencies in interpersonal
functioning. Ladd (1984) points out several possible reasons for
such deficits to be present in children. Some children may lack
specific behaviors in their behavioral repertoires because of inadequate learning or faulty socialization. In this case, social skills
training can be used to help them develop new behaviors. Other
children may begin to lose a particular skill if they have too little
peer interaction to use it sufficiently. If this if the case, social skills
training may be used to strengthen an existing behavior. Some may
have specific social behaviors in their repertoire but fail to use them
because they have learned to substitute other, inappropriate behaviors, or because of interfering emotional factors. Thus, social skills
training can be a means of remediating skill deficits or performance
deficits.

### Development

The earliest effort at developing a theory of social skills training
that is recorded in the literature occurred in 1941. In that year,
Miller and Dollard reviewed existing theories on imitation and for-
mulated their own theory using a behavioral framework. A study

reported by Chittenden in 1942 appears to provide one of the earliest examples of social skills training techniques. Aggressive preschoolers watched doll models who acted nonaggressively and received positive consequences in irritating situations, and doll models who acted aggressively and received unpleasant consequences. Immediately after treatment and at one-month follow-up assessment, children were less domineering and engaged in more cooperative behavior.

The theoretical and empirical work of Albert Bandura (1969) on social learning encouraged a great deal of additional study in the area of social skills training. Bandura found that children who were not exhibiting appropriate social behavior could learn to do so through behavioral procedures such as modeling and differential reinforcement. Bandura (1969) also differentiated between acquisition of a response and performance of that response. He found that an individual who has observed a behavior may not engage in it until he or she believes that performance of the behavior will be reinforced. This finding established the importance of observational learning as well as operant learning. A large number of the studies carried out during the 1970s and 1980s illustrated that social skills training could improve the behavior of children and adolescents with a variety of behavioral problems ranging from aggression to social withdrawal.

## Procedures

Social skills training programs typically focus on teaching skills that are lacking in a child's interpersonal repertoire and that will reduce peer-related problems. The method of choosing specific skills to be taught in a program varies. McFall (1976) specifies four approaches that have been used in the research literature to determine which behaviors to teach in a given program: by fiat, by consensus, the known groups approach, and the empirical method.

When the decision concerning target behaviors is made by fiat, an expert has selected the behavior he or she thinks is appropriate for the client. When the decision is made by consensus, a group of people, such as school psychologists, makes the decision. Ladd (1984) points out that these approaches have been viewed as "adultopomorphic" and are likely to yield behaviors that are not effective in the child's peer group.

The known groups approach involves reliance on the results of studies that examine behaviors used by competent children but not by children with problems. The observed difference between the two groups, however, may not be the difference that accounts for the success of one group and the failure of the other. The empirical method consists of using the results of studies that investigate differences between competent children and children with problems, and then measuring the impact of teaching the behaviors observed to be different on the target child or group.

Three major instructional strategies have been used in social skills training programs: modeling, coaching, and operant learning procedures. When modeling is used, the child learns through observation of social behaviors. When coaching is used, the child is presented with a series of instructions for appropriate behavior and then rehearses the specified behaviors with a coach who provides verbal feedback. Operant learning procedures involve manipulation of events that occur before the target behavior (antecedents) and after the target behavior (consequences). Most social skills training programs use a combination of these methods.

Cartledge and Milburn (1980) provide a detailed description of the steps involved in use of a combination coaching/social modeling program. These include (1) provision of instructions, (2) exposure to a model, (3) rehearsal, (4) performance feedback, and (5) real-life practice.

These authors suggest that children be helped to analyze the components of a social skill themselves instead of being given instructions by an adult. They recommend that the child and the trainer watch a film or read a story depicting children successfully accomplishing a social task, such as making friends, and then, through discussion, identify the specific behavioral responses necessary for successful completion of the task. They emphasize that in specifying behaviors and determining instructions, the trainer should use the words that the child typically uses and should take into account the child's developmental level and cultural characteristics.

Cartledge and Milburn (1980) suggest a variety of methods

that can be used to present models. These include use of puppets, taped models, live models, and models through books. In a review of research on modeling, Bandura (1969) concludes that a model's behavior is more likely to be imitated if the model and the observer are similar in sex, age, race, and attitudes. Models who are viewed as warm, competent, and having prestige, as well as those who are associated with reward to the observer, are also more likely to be imitated.

Goldstein, Sprafkin, and Gershaw (1976) suggest that the modeling presentation be clear and detailed, be ordered from least to most difficult behaviors, have enough repetition, have no irrelevant detail, and use several different models. Use of multiple models increases the probability that the child will learn to use a given set of skills effectively. Multiple models will show variation in behavior and will thereby suggest alternatives to the child and allow for flexibility in behavior. Use of a graduated modeling procedure, in which the model begins performance at a level similar to that of the child observer and gradually progresses to modeling of the behavior at the criterion level, may be helpful in teaching complex or difficult behaviors (Perry & Furukawa, 1980). If the model's behavior is rewarded, the observer is more likely to imitate that behavior.

A behavior that is observed may not be learned unless the child practices the behavior. Behavior rehearsal helps ensure that the child will be able to engage successfully in the target behavior in appropriate situations. Cartledge and Milburn (1980) suggest three methods of conducting behavior rehearsal: through covert responding, through verbal responding, and through motor responding. Covert responding refers to practice through imagery. In this method, the child may be asked to imagine a situation and envision behaving in a particular manner in order to deal with the situation. When verbal responding is used, the child is asked to talk through the situation by describing the scene, how he or she would behave, and possible consequences. Motor responding requires the child to act out the behaviors through role-play.

Feedback is a means of providing information to the child about his or her performance so that necessary corrections can be made. Feedback may be given verbally by the trainer through use of a token or concrete reinforcement system or through use of a self-evaluation system in which the child rates his or her own behavior. Videotapes or audiotapes of the role-play rehearsal session can provide a good basis for encouraging self-evaluation.

The final step in the process is practice in other settings. Once the child has learned to implement a given sequence of social behaviors in simulated situations during role-play activities, practice should occur in a variety of real-life situations. At this point, training sessions should focus on discussion of situations in which the child used the newly learned social skills and the consequences of their use. Alternative behavioral responses can be discussed and rehearsed if the outcome of the response to the situation was not positive.

Arnold Goldstein and his colleagues (Goldstein, Sprafkin, Gershaw, & Klein, 1980) have developed and evaluated a social skills training program, Structured Learning, that has been used successfully with a variety of adolescent populations. Structured Learning consists of four major components: modeling, role-playing, performance feedback, and transfer of training. Through modeling, the adolescent is shown numerous detailed examples of a person performing the target skill, either live, on tape, or on film. Role-playing activities provide the trainee with opportunities to rehearse the skill. Performance feedback provides approval, praise, or instructions for improvement.

Six groups of skills are taught during Structured Learning:

1. Beginning social skills
2. Advanced social skills
3. Skills for dealing with feelings
4. Skill alternatives to aggression
5. Skills for dealing with stress
6. Planning skills

Exhibit 4.1 shows fifty specific skills that these six groups comprise. Each skill is broken down into a series of specific behavioral steps. For example, starting a conversation consists of four steps: (1) greet the other person, (2) make small talk, (3) decide whether the other person is listening, and (4) bring up the main topic. Convincing others involves (1) deciding whether you want to

**Exhibit 4.1. Structured Learning Skills.**

---

*Group 1—Beginning Social Skills*

1. Listening
2. Starting a conversation
3. Having a conversation
4. Asking a question
5. Saying thank you
6. Introducing yourself
7. Introducing other people
8. Giving a compliment

*Group 2—Advanced Social Skills*

9. Asking for help
10. Joining in
11. Giving instructions
12. Following instructions
13. Apologizing
14. Convincing others

*Group 3—Skills for Dealing with Feelings*

15. Knowing your feelings
16. Expressing your feelings
17. Understanding the feelings of others
18. Dealing with someone else's anger
19. Expressing affection
20. Dealing with fear
21. Rewarding yourself

*Group 4—Skill Alternatives to Aggression*

22. Asking permission
23. Sharing something
24. Helping others
25. Negotiating
26. Using self-control
27. Standing up for your rights
28. Responding to teasing
29. Avoiding trouble with others
30. Keeping out of fights

*Group 5—Skills for Dealing with Stress*

31. Making a complaint
32. Answering a complaint
33. Sportsmanship after the game
34. Dealing with embarrassment
35. Dealing with being left out
36. Standing up for a friend
37. Responding to persuasion

Exhibit 4.1. Structured Learning Skills, Cont'd.

---

    38. Responding to failure
    39. Dealing with confusing messages
    40. Dealing with an accusation
    41. Getting ready for a difficult conversation
    42. Dealing with group pressure

*Group 6—Planning Skills*

    43. Deciding on something to do
    44. Deciding on what caused a problem
    45. Setting a goal
    46. Deciding on your abilities
    47. Gathering information
    48. Arranging problems by importance
    49. Making a decision
    50. Concentrating on a task

---

*Source:* From *Skillstreaming the Adolescent: A Structured Learning Approach to Teaching Prosocial Skills* (pp. 84–85) by A. P. Goldstein, R. P. Sprafkin, N. J. Greshaw, and P. Klein, 1980, Champaign, IL: Research Press. Copyright 1980 by the authors. Reprinted by permission.

convince someone about something, (2) telling the other person your idea, (3) asking the other person what he or she thinks about it, (4) telling why you think your idea is a good one, and (5) asking the other person to think about what you said before making up his or her mind.

Goldstein and others (1980) emphasize the importance of transfer of training. This is the trainee's using the skills learned during training in the natural social setting. The authors use a variety of procedures to accomplish this:

1. Providing general principles concerning competent performance
2. Extending learning over more trials than are necessary (over-learning)
3. Making the learning setting, models, and situations similar to what is experienced in real life
4. Using multiple models, trainers, and rehearsal situations (stimulus variability)
5. Setting up supplemental programs outside the Structured

Learning setting to ensure that trainees are provided with reinforcement when they use newly learned social skills

Trainees are also instructed in methods of self-reinforcement (saying positive things to or doing positive things for oneself) when environmental support is insufficient.

Use of operant procedures alone to enhance social skills through manipulation of antecedents has been illustrated by Strain (1977) using a method called peer social initiations. This procedure involves training a peer to initiate positive social interactions with a withdrawn child in a play setting. Manipulating consequences through contingent application of social or token reinforcement can also be an effective means of increasing appropriate social interaction and decreasing aggressive behavior (Allen, Hart, Buell, Harris, & Wolf, 1964). Manipulation of antecedents and consequences has typically been most useful for children with performance rather than skill deficits.

### Assessment Procedures

Social skills of children and adolescents are assessed through six major methods (Elliott, Gresham, & Heffer, 1987):

1. Ratings of significant others (usually teachers or parents)
2. Self-report rating scales
3. Sociometric procedures
4. Behavioral interviews
5. Behavioral role-play measures
6. Observation of performance in the natural environment

Each of these methods provides a different perspective on the child's social behavior. No single measure supplies a complete picture of the child's social functioning or enough information from which to devise an intervention program. Thus, a comprehensive assessment includes multiple measures.

Commercially available rating scales typically yield a global evaluation of behavior. The Child Behavior Checklist (Achenbach & Edelbrock, 1983) is one of the best standardized and validated rating scales available; it includes rating forms to be completed by teachers and parents as well as a self-report form for the child or adolescent. Social competence, withdrawal, and aggression scores can be obtained. The Walker Problem Behavior Identification Checklist (Walker, 1983), the Scale of Social Competence and School Adjustment (Walker & McConnell, 1988), and the Social Skills Rating System (Elliott, Sheridan, & Gresham, 1989) provide somewhat more specific information, given the nature of their individual items and subscales. Through comparison with normative data, these scales also indicate whether a child's social behavior is problematic.

Commercially available scales can be helpful in diagnosing the presence of a social problem and establishing the general type of problem, such as withdrawal or aggression. They do not, however, provide enough specific information about the child's behavior to enable the examiner to pinpoint the behavioral deficit or excess. Cartledge and Milburn (1980) suggest use of examiner-constructed rating scales to obtain information on the specific behaviors that make up a larger social skill to be used in developing a social skills training intervention. To develop such a scale, the examiner must identify the specific, observable behaviors that have to be performed to achieve the desired social goal.

Self-report scales, which are completed by the child or adolescent, can also provide useful information on social behavior, even when the results are not consistent with those gained from rating scales completed by significant others. These reports can identify problem areas resulting from differences in the way the child's behavior is seen by others and by the child himself or herself. For example, a child's problems regarding aggression may be compounded if he or she does not recognize that the problem exists; the initial focus of the intervention would need to address the recognition issue. The Self-Perception Profile for Children (Harter, 1985) and the Matson Evaluation of Social Skills with Youngsters (Matson, Rotatori, & Helsel, 1983) are examples of instruments that focus on obtaining the perceptions of children concerning their own social behavior.

Ratings or nominations of peers are additional sources of valid information concerning a child's social behavior. Such procedures can indicate how well a child is liked or disliked, or the extent to which a child is perceived by peers to have various types of problems.

Behavioral interviewing is another method of obtaining information about a child's social skills, social problems, and social environment; these can all be useful in intervention programming. Such interviews can be conducted with the target child and significant others, such as parents and teachers. From these sources, the interviewer typically attempts to elicit information that will identify target behaviors, point toward current and potential controlling antecedent and consequent stimuli, and assess the mediational potential of parents and teachers.

Direct observation of behavior in the natural setting is one of the most frequently used methods of identifying target behaviors and assessing them in order to plan and evaluate social skills interventions. Direct observation is the process by which an observer records overt motor and/or verbal behavior using an operational definition as a guide (Barton & Ascione, 1984). The observer records the frequency and/or duration of the target behavior. When direct observation procedures are used, observer training and monitoring are necessary to ensure that the results of observation are valid and reliable.

Behavioral role-play tests can furnish an opportunity to observe the child's behavior when observation of the target behavior in the natural social environment is not possible or is impractical. These tests measure social behaviors in contrived settings that are designed to simulate the natural environment in which social problems occur for the child. The tests typically consist of descriptions of social situations with prompts that the child is asked to respond to. The examiner codes the child's verbal and nonverbal responses to the prompt to assess the presence and/or absence of specified behaviors.

## Review of Research

Research on social skills training has focused on effectiveness in dealing with social withdrawal and aggression. Investigators have found that social skills training procedures can be used successfully with a wide age group ranging from preschoolers to adolescents.

A number of studies with very young children have focused on manipulating antecedents and consequences to increase the rate of social interaction in those who are socially isolated and withdrawn. These studies have shown that prompts and contingent reinforcement can be used successfully in the classroom by both adults and peers to increase social interaction. In a relatively early study, Allen, Hart, Buell, Harris, and Wolfe (1964) used positive teacher attention to increase a preschool girl's peer interactions. Subsequently O'Connor (1972) successfully used trained graduate students to shape the behavior of socially isolated preschoolers. The graduate students praised the target children when they interacted with their peers. Studies conducted by Strain and his colleagues (Strain, 1977; Strain, Shores, & Timm, 1977) showed that peers could also be used successfully to prompt and to administer social reinforcement to increase social interaction. Hart, Reynolds, Baer, Brawley, and Harris (1968) shaped cooperative peer interaction through contingent reinforcement from a teacher, demonstrating that adult reinforcement could influence the quality as well as the frequency of social behavior.

Symbolic modeling, in which children are exposed to a film depicting children engaging in the desired social behaviors and being reinforced for doing so, has also been shown to increase social interactions of preschool children (Evers-Pasquale & Sherman, 1975; Jakibchuk & Smeriglio, 1976; O'Connor, 1969, 1972). Cooke and Apolloni (1976) used live modeling to teach social behaviors (smiling, sharing, making positive physical contact, verbal complimenting) to learning disabled elementary school children. One skill was trained at each session, during which the trainer talked briefly about the skill, modeled it, prompted each child to try the behavior, and used praise when the child did so. The investigators observed several results: the target children showed increases not only in the trained behavior but in other positive social behaviors as well; additionally, other children in the classroom increased their positive social behaviors by virtue of their contact with the target children.

Coaching has also been successful in increasing the social interactions of withdrawn children. Whereas operant procedures and modeling have been most effective and used most frequently with preschool children, coaching has been effective with students of elementary school age and older. Whitehill, Hersen, and Bellack (1980) increased the use of specific positive social behaviors of so-cially isolated eight- to ten-year-olds through coaching. The inves-tigators taught the children to ask open-ended questions, make informative statements, and request a shared activity; they used ver-bal instruction of the target skill, adult modeling of the skill, be-havioral rehearsal, and feedback on skill performance. Oden and Asher (1977) used coaching to teach participation, communication, cooperation, and peer reinforcement to third and fourth graders. The coaching procedure consisted of verbal instruction, skill re-hearsal, and performance feedback; the training resulted in in-creases in the children's frequency of positive social interactions and in the sociometric status (peer ratings of likeability) of the target children. Employing similar procedures, Ladd (1981) used coaching with third-grade students who were not well accepted by their class-mates. The researcher coached the target children in asking ques-tions, leading, and offering support to peers. The coached children improved in skill performance and peer acceptance.

The importance of peer involvement in coaching programs has been demonstrated by Bierman and Furman (1984), who taught conversational skills to poorly accepted fifth and sixth graders. The students were assigned to one of four treatment conditions: (1) coaching only, (2) positive peer involvement, (3) combined coach-ing and peer involvement, and (4) no treatment. Students in the coaching condition were trained in self-expression, questioning, and leadership conversational skills. Students in the positive peer involvement condition had the opportunity to interact with peers while making a videotape. Students in the combination condition received skill training within the context of making a film about friends. The coaching and peer involvement conditions had positive but differential effects on the social competence of these children. Only children in the combined treatment condition showed sus-tained improvement in peer acceptance, rate of social interaction, and frequency of conversational skills.

Studies investigating the effectiveness of social skills training with aggressive children have generally been conducted more recently than the studies with withdrawn children. However, a number of the earlier studies that focused on unpopular children failed to distinguish between children who were neglected by others and children who were actively disliked, typically because of aggressive behavior, and thus may have included some aggressive subjects.

Operant procedures have been used in the development of social skills and the concomitant reduction of aggressive behavior through differential reinforcement of other behavior (DRO), in which the child is reinforced for any behavior other than the target, or reinforcing alternative behaviors (ALT-R), in which the child is reinforced for behaviors that offer alternatives to the unwanted behavior (Pinkston, Reese, LeBlanc, & Baer, 1973). The effectiveness of coaching with young aggressive children was demonstrated with elementary school boys in grades 1 to 3 (Bierman, Miller, & Stabb, 1987); this study compared the effectiveness of coaching and response cost (withdrawal of reinforcers as a result of undesirable behavior) on peer interactions and peer ratings. Target skills in the coaching program were (1) questioning others for information, clarification, and invitation; (2) helping, defined as giving support, suggestions, and cooperating in play; and (3) sharing. In addition to conducting the ten half-hour coaching sessions, the trainer, during play activity, praised performance of the skills and rewarded this performance with tokens. The coaching program was found to increase prosocial behaviors but did not decrease negative behaviors; the response cost condition decreased negative behaviors but did not increase prosocial behaviors. The combination treatment, however, produced sustained improvement in increased positive and diminished negative behaviors among the target children and improvement on peer reaction to them. The effectiveness of coaching and modeling has also been demonstrated in a number of studies that used the Structured Learning approach to reduce disruptive and aggressive behavior in adolescents (Goldstein, Sherman, Greshaw, Sprafkin, & Glick, 1978; Greenleaf, 1982).

## Summary

Social skills training programs have been used to help children and adolescents acquire a large variety of social behaviors, thereby increasing peer acceptance while decreasing problems such as social anxiety, withdrawal, or aggression. The programs typically include modeling, coaching, and/or contingent use of reinforcers. They can be conducted by a variety of school support personnel and frequently involve peers in implementation.

A major task for professionals conducting social skills training programs is identifying the social skills that will improve the child's social functioning and peer acceptance as well as the specific behavioral components that make up the target skill. A multimethod approach to assessment can facilitate the diagnostic and intervention planning process.

The most successful programs provide numerous opportunities for the target children to rehearse their newly learned behaviors. Continuing to reward the children in some way is especially important in ensuring maintenance of the new behavior after the initial coaching and modeling components of the training are completed.

*Five*

△

# Acquiring Assertiveness Skills

Assertiveness training is a specific type of social skills training that focuses on teaching the individual "to act in his or her own best interests, to stand up for herself or himself without undue anxiety, to express honest feelings comfortably, or to exercise personal rights without denying the rights of others" (Alberti & Emmons, 1975, p. 27). Assertive behavior is viewed as being the midpoint of a continuum of behavioral styles that range from passive behavior to aggression.

Individuals exhibiting passive behavior avoid confrontations and arguments; they may ignore potentially confrontational situations or give in to others. They fail to express their feelings, thoughts, and beliefs, or they express themselves in such a timid or apologetic manner that they are easily disregarded by others. Individuals behaving in this way can be viewed as violating their own rights. Individuals behaving aggressively, on the other hand, typically become rude, overreact, and attack others. They express themselves in ways that violate the rights of others, and they are often dishonest. The goal of this behavior is typically domination of the other person.

Midway on the behavioral continuum are individuals exhibiting assertive behavior. They stand up for their rights, they express their thoughts, feelings, and beliefs in direct, honest, and appropriate ways, and they do not violate the rights of others. Thus, assertiveness is an approach to social interaction that involves respecting oneself as well as others. In describing assertiveness training for children, Rotheram-Borus (1988) defines assertiveness as "sets of thoughts, feelings, and actions that help a child to obtain personal goals in a socially acceptable manner" (p. 84). This training focuses on teaching individuals, through the use of behavioral procedures, to adopt an assertive style of interacting with others.

## Development

Although reports of interventions similar to assertiveness training appeared in the literature as early as the 1940s (Salter, 1949), Joseph Wolpe (1958) and Arnold Lazarus (Wolpe & Lazarus, 1966) are typically credited with its early development. These authors differentiated assertion from aggression and used role-play procedures as part of their therapeutic intervention with clients. They used assertiveness training to help clients decrease their anxiety related to social interactions.

Major growth in the use and study of assertiveness training occurred after 1970. This interest was spurred by publication of two classic works in the area. *Your Perfect Right,* by Robert Alberti and Michael Emmons (1975), was targeted at a broad audience that included the general public as well as mental health professionals and educators. *Responsible Assertive Behavior,* by Arthur Lange and Patricia Jakubowski (1979), was written for mental health professionals and provided a comprehensive description of the process and its use.

Lange and Jakubowski (1979, p. 2) took a broad approach to defining assertiveness training. They contended that although there was some disagreement in the field, assertiveness training generally incorporated four basic procedures:

"1.    teaching people the differences between assertion and aggression and between nonassertion and politeness;

2.    helping people identify and accept both their own personal rights and the rights of others;

3.    reducing existing cognitive and affective obstacles to acting assertively, e.g., irrational thinking, excessive anxiety, guilt, and anger; and

4.    developing assertive skills through active practice methods."

Although most of the descriptive and empirical literature on assertiveness training deals with adult populations, during the 1970s and 1980s a number of journal articles appeared that described and evaluated use of assertiveness training for a variety of child and adolescent problems, such as passivity, withdrawal, aggression, and anxiety. This type of training has also been used as a preventive approach for general child and adolescent populations and for those who are at risk for substance use.

## Procedures

Lange and Jakubowski (1979) have identified twelve training goals that are essential for successful assertiveness training groups. They contend that although assertiveness training can be done on an individual basis, a group format is advantageous because it gives trainers opportunities during training sessions to interact, exchange ideas, and role-play with others who have similar problems. The literature on assertiveness training with children and adolescents focuses almost exclusively on training in groups.

Lange and Jakubowski's (1979, pp. 4-5) essential training goals include the following:

1.    identify specific situations and behaviors which will be the focus of training;

2.    teach the participants how to ascertain if they have acted assertively rather than aggressively or nonassertively;

3.    help individuals to accept their personal rights and the rights of others;

4. identify and modify the participants' irrational assumptions which produce excessive anxiety and anger and result in nonassertion and aggression;
5. provide opportunities for the participants to practice alternative assertive responses;
6. give specific feedback on how the members could improve their assertive behavior;
7. encourage the members to evaluate their own behavior;
8. positively reinforce successive improvements in assertive behavior;
9. model alternative assertive responses as needed;
10. structure the group procedures so that the members' involvement is widespread and supportive;
11. give considerable permission and encouragement for the participants to behave assertively within and outside of the group; and
12. display leadership behavior which is characterized by assertion rather than aggression or nonassertion.

Lange and Jakubowski (1979) recommend that training occur over six to nine sessions of no more than two hours each. Thirty minutes to one hour for each session is more appropriate for children and adolescents and may necessitate an increased number of sessions.

Training groups are typically either exercise oriented or theme oriented. In exercise-oriented groups, participants can observe and rehearse assertive behavior through a variety of group exercises. For example, in one exercise described by Lange and Jakubowski (1979), group members give and respond to compliments and are encouraged to focus on both verbal and nonverbal behaviors. In other exercises, participants practice carrying on social conversations by asking open-ended questions, responding to information, and paraphrasing. In theme-oriented groups, sessions focus on observation and rehearsal of assertive behavior in a specific type of situation, such as ones in which there is peer pressure to engage in drug or alcohol use or to engage in sexual activity.

Introductory sessions of both types of groups typically provide an overview of the training, information about goals of the group, and a definition of assertiveness as contrasted with passivity and aggression. Descriptions of assertive behavior focus on the non-verbal as well as the verbal components of this type of training. Important nonverbal behaviors include duration of eye contact, duration of speech, loudness of speech, and affect in speech (Eisler, Miller, & Hersen, 1973). Assertive nonverbal behavior consists of an appropriately loud voice, firm eye contact, body gestures that communicate strength, and a fluent speech pattern.

Subsequent sessions typically include a variety of exercises and activities that provide opportunities for group members to observe and practice assertive behaviors through modeling and behavior rehearsal activities. Lange and Jakubowski (1979) enumerate seven behavior rehearsal components that have been used in assertion training:

1. Modeling. The trainee observes another person demonstrating assertive behavior. The model can be the trainer, another group member, a coached actor, or an individual on an audio- or videotape.
2. Covert modeling. The trainee imagines someone behaving assertively in a problem situation.
3. Rehearsal. The trainee practices assertive behaviors with the trainer or other group members in role-play situations.
4. Covert rehearsal. The trainee imagines himself or herself behaving assertively in a problem situation.
5. Role reversal. In a role-play activity, the trainee takes the part of the individual responding to another person who is behaving assertively and thus experiences being the receiver of assertive behavior.
6. Reinforcement. The trainer and other group members give positive reinforcement to an individual who is practicing assertive behaviors.
7. Coaching. The trainer and group members provide specific descriptions of the components of an assertive behavior.

Rotheram (1980) provides a description of an assertiveness training program for use with third to sixth graders. Training with this program typically spans twelve to twenty weeks. Training methods include didactic instruction, shaping, and behavioral rehearsal procedures. There is a focus on skill development in meeting other people, complimenting others, and handling anger.

The training format involves dividing a class of children into teams of six to twelve. Each of these teams is then divided into "actors" and "directors," with a paraprofessional leader or "supercoach." The supercoach presents the actors with an interpersonal problem. The actors then use problem solving to come up with a solution to the situation, and rehearse the solution through role-playing. The actors receive feedback from the directors in the form of tokens.

The content of Rotheram's (1980) program is divided into seven phases. Each phase includes didactic instruction and role-playing, and addresses nonverbal behaviors, interpersonal problem-solving activities, and thought rehearsal. In the first phase, students learn the difference between passive, assertive, and aggressive behavior. The second phase focuses on identifying feelings, specifically anxiety, associated with social situations. In addition, during this phase, students are taught simple relaxation techniques for use in dealing with anxiety. Phase three focuses on giving and receiving compliments and using positive self-statements. During phase four, students practice making friends through asking open questions that require more than one-word answers. Phases five and six focus on coping with criticism and dealing with anger through use of self-statements and appropriate behavioral responses. During the final phase, the focus is on integration of thinking, feeling, and acting assertively.

Rotheram-Borus (1988) reports that integration of thinking, feeling, and acting can be practiced using the following sequence:

1. Identify the problem.
2. Set a positive goal.
3. Assess your feelings.
4. Relax by encouraging yourself, spelling your name backward, or tensing and relaxing your muscles.
5. Generate alternative ways to achieve your goal; evaluate these alternatives and select one.

6.  Identify your successes.
7.  Decide what to do next time.

Rotheram (1980) describes similar programs appropriate for implementation with adolescents. A program for ninth graders focuses on assertiveness issues related to parents and teachers, while a program for twelfth graders focuses on peer relationships and dating. The training format for both programs includes didactic instruction and role-play experiences.

In a recent report, Rotheram-Borus (1988) reiterates the idea that assertiveness requires an interaction of cognitive, affective, and behavioral skills. She enumerates four principles, based on social learning theory, that should guide this approach to coping skills development:

1.  Emphasize and reward strengths. This can be accomplished through verbal praise and use of tokens.
2.  Use successive approximations in efforts at teaching new behavior. This can be accomplished by presenting information in small chunks and setting gradually increased goals for behavior change.
3.  Model assertive behavior. Trainers should model thought processes and emotional coping processes associated with assertiveness as well as verbal and nonverbal assertive behaviors.
4.  Encourage independent thinking. To accomplish this goal, a trainer should build experiences into the training session in which students critically analyze their own behavior and that of their peers after role-play exercises.

### Specialized Assessment Instruments

A few self-report scales have been developed to assess assertiveness in children; one of these is the Wood and Michelson (1978) Children's Assertive Behavior Scale (CABS), a multiple-choice instrument that measures a variety of behaviors related to assertiveness. The scale consists of twenty-seven items that provide brief descriptions of social situations. The child is asked to indicate how he or she would respond to each situation, and each response has a corresponding assertiveness value that ranges from very passive to very aggressive. The items represent five areas: conversation skills, responses to compliments, complaints, requests, and empathy. Below is an example of one item.

> Someone says to you, "I think you are a very nice person."
>
> You would usually:
>
> 1. Say, "No, I'm not that nice." (very passive)
> 2. Say, "Yes, I think I am the best!" (very aggressive)
> 3. Say, "Thank you." (assertive)
> 4. Say nothing and blush. (passive)
> 5. Say, "Thanks, I am really great." (aggressive)

This scale has a parallel form to be completed by teachers, who rate the child on the same items, indicating what the child would typically do in the situation specified by the item. Adequate internal consistency and four-week test-retest reliability have been established for this instrument. The scale has also been found to be sensitive to the effects of assertiveness training programs (Michelson & Wood, 1982).

The Rathus Assertiveness Scale Revised for Children (Michelson & Wood, 1982) is an additional self-report scale consisting of thirty-eight items to which the child is asked to indicate agreement or disagreement. This scale includes items such as "I like to argue," and "I won't hurt somebody's feelings, even if they hurt mine."

Connor, Dann, and Twentyman (1982) describe the development of a self-report measure of assertiveness for young adolescents, the Adolescent Assertion Expression Scale (AAES). In developing this scale, the authors used Alberti and Emmons's (1975) conceptualization of assertiveness (the ability to express one's thoughts and feelings without violating the rights of others). The scale contains sixty items, some of which were modified from adult assertiveness scales. Students are asked to indicate the extent to which each of the items describes them. In assessing the validity of the scale, the authors found that the self-reports of assertiveness were corroborated by teacher ratings of the students' assertiveness and by ratings of the students obtained during a behavioral role-play test.

There have also been some efforts to develop behavioral analogue situation tests that assess assertiveness. One example of this is the Behavioral Assertiveness Test for Children (BAT-C; Bornstein, Bellack, & Hersen, 1977). The test consists of nine role-play situations in which an assertive response would be appropriate. The situations are presented verbally by a narrator. A confederate in the room provides a prompt at the end of the narration to initiate a response by the child. An example of one of the situations is as follows.

*Narrator:*   You're in school and you brought your chair to another classroom to watch a movie. You go out to get a drink of water. When you come back Mike is sitting in your seat.

*Prompt:*   I'm sitting here.

The scenes are videotaped and the child's response is scored later for three behavior categories: ratio of eye contact to speech duration, loudness of speech, and requests for new behavior. In addition, an overall rating of assertiveness is made.

## Review of Research

The research literature on the effectiveness of assertiveness training programs with children and adolescents is not extensive; however, a number of these studies document positive effects resulting from this approach. The studies have focused on both prevention and treatment and have targeted a number of emotions and behaviors, including assertive behavior, self-esteem, aggression and other school discipline problems, anxiety, and substance use.

Rotheram (1980) has evaluated the programs for elementary school children described above. Two hundred eighty fourth and fifth graders participated in the study. When compared to students in a no-treatment control group, students who participated in the training had increases in scores on measures of problem solving and assertiveness, teacher ratings of popularity, and grades; they had decreases in scores on teacher ratings of behavior problems.

In a subsequent report, Rotheram and her colleagues (Rotheram, Armstrong, & Booraem, 1982) describe the evaluation of an assertiveness training program conducted with 343 fourth and fifth graders. The training procedures were administered in one-hour sessions twice per week for twelve weeks to groups of six students each. The groups were conducted in the following sequence:

1. A specific assertiveness concept or technique was presented.
2. The group leader presented problem situations (for example, "You are in a market, every line is long and you have one item. What can you do?" [p. 570]).
3. The group generated alternative solutions to the problem.
4. Group members role-played solutions to the problem situations and received feedback on their behavior in the form of tokens that indicated whether the behavior was passive, aggressive, or assertive.

After participating in this training, students showed increases in assertiveness, improved grades, and more favorable teacher ratings of behavior when compared with students in control intervention groups and a no-treatment control group.

In an additional study with third graders, Vogrin and Kassinove (1979) examined the effects of an assertiveness training program consisting of sixteen 40-minute sessions. Two types of programs, one including behavioral rehearsal and the other using audiotaped models without behavioral rehearsal, were compared to a condition in which children received attention only and to a no-treatment control condition. The assertiveness training programs resulted in improvements on assertiveness measures; the program including behavioral rehearsal had the most positive effects, illustrating the importance of this component of the training.

The programs for adolescents described by Rotheram (1980) were evaluated in studies with twenty-six ninth graders and thirty-four twelfth graders. Members of groups rated by the adolescent participants themselves as cohesive had increases in assertiveness on behavioral and self-report measures as well as decreases in teacher ratings of behavior problems, compared to students in noncohesive assertiveness training groups and no-treatment control groups. Positive results of a program for adolescents that focused on increasing assertiveness were also reported by Waksman (1984). In this study, twenty-three adolescents in a middle school health science class, who participated in thirteen 45-minute sessions over one month, made changes on measures of self-concept and locus of control when compared to those who received no training.

The studies described above indicate that assertiveness training can be effective in improving the social coping skills of general populations of school-aged children and adolescents. Additional studies have documented the effectiveness of assertiveness training in dealing with children and youth who are at risk for or who have specific emotional and/or behavioral problems.

In an early study, Bornstein, Bellack, and Hersen (1977) examined the effects of assertiveness training on four unassertive children, ranging in age from eight to eleven, who were described by their teachers as excessively cooperative, passive, shy, unassertive, and conforming, and who met the criteria of at least three deficient verbal and nonverbal behaviors (poor eye contact, short speech duration, inaudible responses, inability to make requests) during baseline assessment. The children received three weeks of training, with three 15- to 30-minute sessions per week. The training focused on increasing the children's eye contact, loudness and duration of speech, and number of requests. Training procedures included feedback on performance, modeling, and rehearsal. The training resulted in improvement in individual assertive behaviors as well as overall assertiveness for all four children.

A recent study has examined the effectiveness of assertiveness training in modifying the aggressive behavior of young children (Tanner & Holliman, 1988). In this investigation, the subjects were twenty-four first through third graders who were nominated by their teachers because of frequent teasing, pushing, hitting, fighting, arguing, exploding in outbursts of temper, or demonstrating difficulty in sharing or taking turns. Children participated in a three-week training group meeting twice weekly for one hour. Training focused on recognizing and differentiating assertive, aggressive, and passive responses and practicing assertive responses; it also included cognitive and physiological control techniques to use in anger-provoking situations. This study offered limited support for the effectiveness of the training program as the children improved on only a few of the measures used, including one measure of cooperation and one measure of physical aggression.

Other studies targeting aggressive behavior of adolescents have yielded more positive results (Huey, 1983; Huey & Rank, 1984; Pentz, 1980). Huey and Rank (1984) examined the effectiveness of assertiveness training with eighth- and ninth-grade black males who attended an urban high school. The students who participated in the training were randomly selected from a pool of students referred by their teachers for chronic classroom disruption. These students also had low academic skills and family income level. The training was conducted over eight hours, with groups meeting twice a week for four weeks. Results indicated that both counselor-led and peer-led groups showed increases in assertive skills and decreases in classroom aggressive behavior, while control groups showed no change.

The effects of assertiveness training on anxiety have also been examined in a study conducted with highly anxious adolescents (Wehr & Kaufman, 1987). Subjects in this study were ninth graders who showed extreme anxiety according to scores on an anxiety scale, who had an IQ of 68 or above, and whose achievement scores were less than two years below grade level in reading and mathematics. Assertiveness training was conducted for two class periods a week for two weeks, and included lectures, discussion, modeling, role-playing, behavior rehearsal, coaching, and feedback. Adolescents who participated in the training scored significantly higher on an assertiveness measure and significantly lower on a scale that measures situational anxiety when compared to a placebo control group, but the training had no effect on academic achievement.

A few studies have examined the effects of assertiveness training on self-esteem of adolescents. Stake, DeVille, and Pennell (1983) found a twelve-hour assertiveness training program to be effective in improving the self-esteem of high school girls who entered the program with low scores on a self-esteem measure. However, in a study of the effects of assertiveness training on the self-esteem of black high school students, Stewart and Lewis (1986) found increases in assertive behavior for females but not for males, and no effect on self-esteem as a result of the ten-session training program.

Positive effects have been found when assertiveness training is used as an approach to prevent or decrease alcohol and other drug use in adolescents. Horan and Williams (1982) conducted five 45-minute assertiveness training sessions over a two-week period with nonassertive junior high school students. The training focused on situations requiring general assertiveness and those specifically involving peer pressure to use drugs. The seventy-two students who participated in this study were assigned randomly to the assertiveness training treatment, a placebo treatment, or a no-treatment control group. The ones who participated in assertiveness training showed significant gains on self-reported and behavioral measures of assertiveness and a decreased willingness to use alcohol and marijuana. At three-year follow-up assessment, the positive effects on assertiveness for this group were maintained, and they also showed less actual drug use than students in no-treatment or placebo control conditions. Other studies in which assertiveness training has been used as one component of coping skills training have produced similarly positive results with respect to alcohol and other drug use (Botvin & Wills, 1985). However, such positive effects were not achieved in a study conducted by Del Greco, Breitbach, Rumer, McCarthy, and Suissa (1986); these researchers found no effects of training on assertiveness or smoking behavior of seventh graders in health education classes.

Use of assertiveness training with children of separation and divorce has also been investigated, although only one study has been completed in this area. Roseby and Deutsch (1985) found that ten weeks of group counseling, including training in social role-taking and assertive communication, resulted in positive effects on the fourth- and fifth-grade participants' attitudes and beliefs about their parents' divorce, but no changes in participants' depression or school behavior.

In summary, assertiveness training has been examined as both a preventive and a treatment approach to child and adolescent emotional and behavioral problems. Positive effects have been found regarding the potential of this training to increase assertive behavior in general populations of children and adolescents and those who are identified as unassertive. However, the concurrent effects on general adjustment are less clear. The few studies that have examined effects on specific problem areas, such as self-esteem, show more success when the problem emotional or behavioral area is documented in the child or adolescent. Anxiety, aggression, and substance use appear to be problem areas that show the greatest potential for positive impact as a result of assertiveness training, according to the extant literature.

## Summary

Assertiveness training can provide an effective means of teaching children and adolescents social coping skills that promote the individual's goals without violating the rights of others. Although some positive results have been reported in this area, the number of evaluative studies completed is extremely small. Evidence of effectiveness, therefore, is by no means conclusive. The most positive results have occurred when this type of training has been used as a preventive measure for general school populations and as a way to help youth deal with anxiety and aggression and to resist peer pressure to use alcohol and other drugs.

Much, however, remains to be discovered about appropriate implementation of this type of training. Most studies conducted to date have used individuals trained in therapy or counseling to implement training procedures. The study cited above conducted by Huey and Rank (1984) indicates that peer-led groups have the potential for producing positive change in a cost-effective manner. The effectiveness of the classroom teacher in implementing these procedures remains to be determined. In addition, the optimal length for training has not been established and the extent to which the effects of training can be maintained remains largely unexplored.

An additional issue that needs further exploration relates to the increasing cultural diversity of our nation's schools. The tenets of assertiveness training are based on behavior that is acceptable in a white middle-class cultural setting (Rotheram-Borus, 1988). The assertive behaviors that have been identified by previous research in this area are appropriate to the white middle class; their acceptability to other cultural groups is still to be determined. As school populations become more culturally diverse, the advisability of teaching children and adolescents to behave in one manner in the school setting while their home and neighborhood settings require other behaviors for success is an important issue that needs further study.

*Six*

<br>

△
△△

# Using
# Self-Instruction Techniques

Children and adolescents can deal with a variety of potentially stressful situations by controlling their own emotional, social, and academic behaviors through use of verbal self-instructions, also called self-statements. Self-instruction training, which has been used to teach this type of coping skill, focuses on teaching individuals to interrupt themselves before they perform an inappropriate behavior and to guide their behavior through use of internal dialogue. Self-instruction training has been used most frequently with children and adolescents who have problems with hyperactivity, impulsiveness, and aggression. It has also been used to improve academic skills in reading and mathematics and to enhance creativity.

## Development

Self-instruction training procedures were first developed by Donald Meichenbaum in the early and mid-1970s. Meichenbaum built on the theoretical work of the Soviet psychologists Luria (1961) and Vygotsky (1962), who described how voluntary motor behaviors of children could be controlled by the verbal behavior, first of others and later of the children themselves. These self-regulating verbalizations were hypothesized to be first overt and later covert.

Using this theoretical framework, Meichenbaum and Goodman (1971) developed and evaluated one of the first self-instruction training programs for children. This program was designed for impulsive children with the goal of teaching them to use self-statements to control behavior. It consisted of five steps: (1) cognitive modeling—the trainer performed a task while self-instructing out loud; (2) overt, external guidance—the child performed the same task while the model gave instructions; (3) overt self-guidance—the child performed the task while self-instructing out loud; (4) faded, overt self-guidance—the child performed the task while whispering self-instructions; and (5) covert self-instruction— the child performed the task while using private speech regarding self-direction. The content of the verbalizations consisted of questions about the nature and demands of the task, answers to these questions that focused on planning, statements that helped the child guide his or her behavior to task completion, and self-reinforcing statements. Following is an example of the content of the self-statements used in this study.

> Okay, what is it I have to do? You want me to copy the picture with the different lines. I have to go slow and be careful. Okay, draw the line down, down, good; then to the right, that's it; now down some more and to the left. Good, I'm doing fine so far. Remember go slow. Now back up again. No, I was supposed to go down. That's okay. Just erase the line carefully. . . . Good. Even if I make an error I can go on slowly and carefully. Okay, I have to go down now. Finished. I did it [Meichenbaum & Goodman, 1971, p. 117].

A variety of tasks were used in training the subjects in this study, impulsive second graders, to use self-instructions. These ranged from simple sensorimotor tasks, such as copying line patterns and coloring figures, to complex problem-solving tasks such as solving items from the Raven's Matrices test (Raven, 1960). Compared to students in the control group, children in the self-instruction training group improved significantly on the Porteus Maze test (Porteus, 1955), the Wechsler Intelligence Scale for Children (WISC) (Wechsler, 1949), and the Matching Familiar Figures Test (Kagan, 1966). The improvement was maintained at one-month follow-up.

Subsequent to this study, a number of researchers and practitioners began exploring the use of self-instruction training with a variety of childhood and adolescent problems. Problem areas in which self-instruction training has been applied include hyperactivity, impulsivity, aggression, disruptive classroom behavior, cheating, school attendance, and academic performance.

### Procedures

Kendall and Braswell (1985) outlined the standard content of most self-instruction training programs. They indicated that self-instructions are designed to help children identify a problem, initiate a strategy for reaching a solution, consider options, and take action on a chosen plan.

To achieve these goals, most self-instruction training programs teach children to generate self-statements related to six phases. The first is problem definition. During this phase the child uses self-statements that help identify the problem and its relevant features. The second is problem approach. During this phase the child uses self-statements that define a strategy for dealing with the problem. During the third phase, focusing of attention, the child reminds him- or herself to concentrate on the problem and the problem-solving strategies to be used. During the next phase, choosing an answer, the child may self-instruct to narrow problem solving to one particular strategy. Finally, as a result of the problem-solving actions completed, the child uses either self-reinforcing statements or coping statements. Through self-reinforcing statements the child recognizes success in addressing the problem situation. Through coping statements the child can address constructively his or her failure to deal with the problem situation and can resolve to confront the problem the next time it arises. Table 6.1

**Table 6.1. Contents of Self-Instructions.**

| | |
|---|---|
| Problem definition: | "Let's see, what am I supposed to do?" |
| Problem approach: | "I have to look at all the possibilities." |
| Focusing of attention: | "I better concentrate and focus in, and think only of what I'm doing right now." |
| Choosing an answer: | "I think it's this one . . ." |
| Self-reinforcement: | "Hey, not bad. I really did a good job." |
| or | |
| Coping statement: | "Oh, I made a mistake. Next time I'll try and go slower and concentrate more and maybe I'll get the right answer." |

*Source:* Kendall & Braswell, 1985, p. 120.

provides illustrations of self-statements from each of the phases described above.

Kendall and Braswell (1985, pp. 182–183) provide the following example of a therapist's explanation to a child of use of verbal self-instructions.

Now let's talk about the five things or steps that we shall be saying out loud each time we do a task or problem. At first it may be hard to remember them all, but we shall practice them together so you will know what to say.

The first thing to say to yourself is, "What am I supposed to do?" We say that so we can be sure we are doing the right problem in the right way.

The second thing we say is, "Look at all the possibilities." That means be sure to look at all the different answers so we can find the best possible one.

Next, we'll be telling ourselves to "focus in." That way we remind ourselves to really concentrate or think hard about just the problem we are working on right now. We don't need to look at or think about anything else.

The fourth step is to pick an answer after studying the different choices or possibilities.

And, finally, the fifth step is to check out our answer and if we got it right we tell ourselves that we did a good job. If we didn't get it right, we don't have to put ourselves down, but we could remind ourselves to be more careful or go more slowly on the next task.

Bash and Camp (1980) describe a self-instruction training program called the Think Aloud program designed for use with aggressive children. The main focus of the program is to teach children to use self-statements to guide problem solving and behavior. The program consists of twenty-three lessons that can be used in a therapeutic or preventive manner. The program combines the self-instructional training approach with the social problem-solving approach described in Chapter Three. The first part of the program addresses development of an organized approach to problem solving. The approach uses four questions: (1) What is my problem? or What am I supposed to do? (2) How can I do it? or What is my plan? (3) Am I using my plan? (4) How did I do? Students learn to use these questions through practice with a variety of cognitive problems and materials beginning with simple ones such as coloring and progressing to more complex problems such as mazes. When this approach is mastered with cognitive problems, the skills are applied to social problems.

Kendall and Braswell (1985) indicate that use of behavioral contingencies along with training in self-instruction is essential for program success. They suggest use of four types of procedures: self-reward and social reward, response cost, self-evaluation, and rewarded homework assignments.

As indicated previously, children are typically taught to make positive statements congratulating themselves on their problem-solving successes as part of the self-instruction sequence. In addition, positive verbal comments and nonverbal gestures should be used by the trainer to augment self-rewards.

A number of researchers and practitioners have added a response-cost procedure to training in use of self-instructions to help the child learn and apply the self-instructional approach to problem solving. In response-cost procedures, the child is given a number of tokens before the training begins and told that tokens can be taken away for specific reasons such as answering a question incorrectly or forgetting one of the self-instruction steps. If a token is taken away, the child is given an explanation that may cue improved future performance. At the end of a training session or other interval the child can trade retained tokens for a concrete or activity reward.

Children are taught self-evaluation skills so they can evaluate their own behavior outside the training setting or classroom environment where behavioral contingencies provide external control of behavior. They can learn to rate their daily behavior on a chart, with ratings ranging from "not so good" to "super." This can be accomplished by first having the trainer rate the child's behavior and provide an explanation of the rating to the child at the end of each training session. In later sessions, the trainer and the child would each independently rate the child's behavior for the session and then compare ratings. The child would be rewarded for ratings that were consistent with those of the trainer. Using this method, children can learn to evaluate themselves accurately.

Homework assignments are used to encourage the child to use self-instructions outside the training setting. They also provide a way to move the child gradually from use of self-instructions in relatively simple problem situations to use in complex problem situations. Appropriate use of self-instructions outside the training setting can be rewarded through a token system by the trainer.

Meichenbaum (1977) has suggested that the trainer introduce children to use of self-instructions through a play situation prior to engaging them in formal training with training manuals or trainer-constructed tasks. Through parallel play with a child, the trainer can model use of self-instructions and then begin training on a set of games in which the child is probably proficient. In other observations about implementation of self-instruction training programs, Meichenbaum (1977) emphasizes the importance of using words that are appropriate for the child's developmental level and likely to be used by the child in the natural social environment. In addition, he underscores the importance of using affect in self-verbalizations, as opposed to repeating the self-instructions in a mechanical fashion without inflections that indicate meaning.

A few studies have provided some direction for the practitioner regarding the content of the verbal self-instructions used in self-instruction training. Kendall and Wilcox (1980) compared the use of "conceptual" versus "concrete" instructions with non-self-controlled third to sixth graders. Examples of conceptual instructions, which are global and abstract, and concrete instructions, which are task specific, can be seen in Exhibit 6.1. These investigators found that the group trained with conceptual instructions made greater improvements in response rate, errors, behavioral self-

**Exhibit 6.1. Concrete Versus Conceptual Self-Instructions.**

*Concrete Self-Instructions*

Problem Definition: I'm to find the picture that doesn't match.
Problem Approach: This one's a clock, this one's a clock.
Focusing of Attention: Look at the pictures.
Self-Reinforcement: The cup and saucer is different; (check answer sheet) I got it right. Good job!
Coping Statement: Oh, it's not the clock that's different, it's the teacup. I can pick out the correct one next time.
Response-Cost Labeling: (done by the trainer) No, it's not the clock, it's the teacup. You lose one chip for picking the clock.

*Conceptual Self-Instructions*

Problem Definition: My first step is to make sure I know what I'm supposed to do.
Problem Approach: Well, I should look at all the possibilities.
Focusing of Attention: I should think about only what I'm doing right now.
Self-Reinforcement: (checking the answer sheet) Hey, good job. I'm doing very well.
Coping Statement: Well, if I make a mistake I can remember to think more carefully next time, and then I'll do better.
Response-Cost Labeling: (done by the trainer) No, that's not the right answer. You lost one token for not taking your time and getting the correct answer.

*Source:* Kendall, P. C., & Wilcox, L. E. (1980). A cognitive-behavioral treatment for impulsivity: Concrete versus conceptual training in non-self-controlled problem children. *Journal of Consulting and Clinical Psychology, 48,* 85. Copyright 1980 by the American Psychological Association. Reprinted by permission.

control, and hyperactivity ratings than did the group trained with concrete instructions. In addition, Copeland (1981) has examined age-related differences and suggests that young children need specific instructions, while older children (eight and over) can benefit from more general concepts.

The self-reinforcement component of self-instruction training received special attention in a study conducted by Nelson and Birkimer (1978) with black, cognitively impulsive second and third graders. These investigators found significant improvement for students who participated in self-instruction training with self-reinforcement, while those receiving self-instruction training without self-reinforcement did not improve.

### Specialized Assessment Instruments

A few task performance measures and behavior rating scales have been used frequently in studies evaluating the effectiveness of self-instruction training programs. Despite their frequent use, these measures do not directly assess the acquisition of self-instruction skills.

The Matching Familiar Figures Test (MFFT) (Kagan, 1966) uses twelve items to measure the extent to which an individual is reflective (slow and accurate) or impulsive (fast and inaccurate) in responding to the test items. The child is shown a picture of a familiar object and is asked to identify the identical picture from among six choices that are variations of the object. A latency score and an error score are obtained from this measure. Improvements on these scores are thought to indicate improvement in self-control and have therefore been used in a number of studies that have evaluated treatment effects of self-instruction training (Kendall & Braswell, 1985).

The Porteus Maze Test (Porteus, 1955) consists of a series of paper-and-pencil mazes that are designed to measure planning, foresight, impulsivity, and distractibility. This test yields a test quotient (TQ), an index of ability to solve the mazes in a specified number of trials, and a qualitative score (Q), based on the number of errors committed while solving the mazes.

The Self-Control Rating Scale (SCRS) (Kendall & Wilcox,

1979) was developed to assess self-control in elementary school children through teacher and/or parent ratings. It is based on a cognitive-behavioral conceptualization of self-control that includes skills in generating and evaluating alternatives, inhibiting unwanted behavior, and engaging in desired behavior. The instrument consists of thirty-three items that are rated on a seven-point scale. Kendall and his colleagues have found that the SCRS is sensitive to the effects of cognitive-behavioral interventions, such as self-instruction training, and that scores parallel changes in observed classroom behavior (Kendall & Braswell, 1982; Kendall & Wilcox, 1980; Kendall & Zupan, 1981.)

To assess self-instruction skills more directly, Meichenbaum (1977) has suggested that the practitioner use projective-type measures in which the child's response to a particular story or role-play situation is analyzed for specific kinds of verbalizations. The subject is shown a picture of a scene depicting a problem situation and is then asked to describe what the child in the picture was thinking and feeling, as well as what the subject would do to handle the situation.

## Review of Research

Research on self-instruction training programs has focused on modification of children's impulsive and aggressive behavior. Subsequent to the 1971 Meichenbaum and Goodman study described previously, a number of other researchers investigated the effectiveness of this approach.

Douglas, Parry, Marton, and Garson (1976) examined the effectiveness of a self-instruction training program that consisted of modeling, self-instructive verbalizations, and self-reinforcement. The twenty-nine six- to ten-year-old hyperactive boys who participated in the program were seen for twenty-four sessions of one hour each, twice per week for three months. The children in the treatment group observed an adult model who, while engaging in a task, verbalized statements about the nature of the task and strategies used. The children then engaged in similar tasks and were asked to imitate the model's verbalizations. The children's verbalizations were gradually faded to covert levels in which they were talking to themselves. The training used a wide variety of tasks and games, both cognitive and social, including some that were assigned by the child's teacher. Strategies emphasized in the training included defining the problem, evaluating alternative solutions before responding, checking one's work, calmly correcting errors, and reinforcing oneself for success. The children worked both alone and in pairs to simulate situations in the classroom environment. The trainer also met with each child's teacher at least six times and each child's parents at least twelve times to familiarize them with the training techniques and encourage them to implement the training program in the classroom and at home. Members of the treatment group improved significantly, relative to the control group, on measures of cognitive style, affective reactions to frustration, perceptual-motor functioning, and listening comprehension. Improvements were maintained at three-month follow-up assessment.

Kendall and Braswell (1982) conducted another notable study of the effectiveness of self-instruction training with twenty-seven children between eight and twelve years old who had been referred by their teachers for exhibiting non-self-controlled behavior. The children were seen for forty-five minutes, twice per week, for a total of twelve sessions. Those in the self-instruction training group were taught five self-instructional problem-solving steps: defining the problem, approaching the problem, focusing attention, selecting an answer, and self-reinforcement or coping with failure. As in the 1976 study by Douglas and others, the trainer first modeled the verbalizations while engaging in a task; the child was then asked to imitate the trainer's behavior and gradually to fade the volume of the verbal self-instructions. Children were initially instructed to use self-instructions that were concrete in nature, changing over time to those that were conceptual or more abstract (see Exhibit 6.1). Training was performed with tasks that were cognitive and academic (for example, math problems) as well as with tasks of a social/emotional nature (such as identifying emotions of others). A response-cost contingency was also implemented during the training; this allowed children to be fined tokens for using the self-instruction steps incorrectly but also to earn bonus tokens for employing self-instruction strategies at home or in school or for accurately evaluating their own performance during the training session.

The children who participated in this training improved significantly on teacher ratings of self-control, children's self-concept data, and off-task behavior relative to a behavioral treatment group and an attention control group. This effect persisted at ten-week follow-up. However, both the self-instruction training group and the behavioral treatment group, which was exposed to the same training tasks and behavioral contingencies, improved on teacher ratings of hyperactivity, cognitive style, and spelling and math achievement. No differences between groups were found for reading achievement or parent ratings of self-control or hyperactivity. Unfortunately, significant group differences did not maintain at one-year follow-up. However, the authors concluded that self-instruction training can make a positive contribution to a cognitive-behavioral treatment program.

The Think Aloud program, described previously, has been evaluated in several studies (Camp, 1980; Camp & Bash, 1980; Camp, Blom, Hebert, & van Doorninck, 1977) with aggressive children. This program has resulted in changes in paper-and-pencil measures of problem solving and impulsivity, but evidence of decreases in actual aggressive behavior has not been documented.

Researchers who have reviewed studies on the effectiveness of self-instruction training (Kendall & Braswell, 1985; Whalen, Henker, & Henshaw, 1985; Hughes, 1988) have concluded that self-instruction training programs have demonstrated short-term effectiveness with students who have problems with impulsivity and self-control. They have also concluded, however, that no effectiveness has been demonstrated in decreasing aggressive, acting-out behavior. Kendall and Braswell (1985) suggest that interventions involving a great deal of trainer/child interaction, child involvement in development of the training/treatment process, and behavioral contingencies produce the greatest gains.

In a meta-analysis of forty-eight outcome studies that applied self-statement modification to childhood behavior disorders, Dush, Hirt, and Schroeder (1989) found positive effects. They also discovered that programs conducted in clinical settings, such as special education programs or outpatient clinics, tended to be more effective than those conducted in regular school settings; that therapist experience had a strong, positive relationship to outcome, with doctoral-level therapists associated with outcomes over seven times larger than those of therapists without graduate training; that at least five to eight hours of training were necessary to produce positive effects; and that long-term effects of this treatment had not been demonstrated. They called for expansion of studies to areas other than impulsivity and disruptive behavior.

## Summary

Self-instruction training teaches children to use self-verbalizations as a means of guiding their behavior. Meichenbaum (1979) suggests a number of guidelines that should be used in developing and implementing effective self-instruction training programs with young children. These include the following:

1. Play should be used to initiate and model self-talk.
2. Tasks selected for the program should be likely to engender use of sequential cognitive strategies.
3. Peer teaching can be initiated by having non-target children do cognitive modeling.
4. Children should be allowed to move through the program at their own rate; the training should include problem-solving statements as well as coping and self-reinforcing statements.
5. The trainer should guard against use of self-statements by the target children in a mechanical, noninvolved fashion.
6. The trainer should be animated and responsive.
7. The child should learn to use verbal self-instructions with low-intensity responses.
8. Self-instruction training should be supplemented with imagery techniques (see Chapter Two).
9. The training should be supplemented with operant procedures such as a response-cost (token) system.

Self-instruction training programs are used most frequently and most effectively with elementary school–aged children who have problems with self-control or impulsivity. This approach can be used with individual students or in small group interventions. Although the approach is described extensively in the literature and appears straightforward and simple to implement, research suggests that therapeutic skill and sophistication may be needed to obtain positive outcomes (Dush et al., 1989). The practitioner should also be cognizant of the lack of demonstrated long-term effects of this approach; therefore, procedures designed to maintain gains resulting from the initial training should be an integral part of the intervention program.

*Seven*

# Decreasing Irrational Beliefs

As stated in Chapter One, the way a person perceives a potential stressor has a direct effect on that person's response to the stressor. Rational-emotive therapy and education procedures, initially developed by Albert Ellis, have been used to help both normal and disturbed children and adolescents learn to deal constructively with potential stressors. The rational-emotive approach is based on the idea that thoughts and beliefs have a direct influence on emotions and behavior. More specifically, the rational-emotive approach identifies a number of beliefs commonly held in our culture that lead to unconstructive emotional and behavioral reactions; it disputes these beliefs and provides alternative, rational ways of thinking that can be used to help individuals lead more satisfying, constructive lives.

## Development

Rational-emotive therapy (RET) was developed by Albert Ellis in the mid-1950s, initially for use with adults. In the late 1960s and

1970s, a number of descriptive and empirical reports began to appear in the psychological and educational literature suggesting that rational-emotive procedures could be used with children and adolescents with a variety of emotional and behavioral problems. These included conduct disorders, low frustration tolerance, impulsivity, anxiety, social isolation, depression, obesity, sexual problems, and academic underachievement (Ellis & Bernard, 1983). In 1970, the Living School, a small private elementary school where children were taught RET along with the regular school curriculum, was started by the Institute for Rational-Emotive Therapy in New York (Bernard & Joyce, 1984). In 1974, William Knaus, consulting psychologist to the Living School, published *Rational-Emotive Education: A Manual for Elementary School Teachers,* which seems to have been responsible for a substantial increase in the use of rational-emotive procedures in school settings. During the 1970s and 1980s a sizable body of literature emerged documenting the use of the rational-emotive approach for therapeutic and preventive intervention not only with children and adolescents but also with their significant others, such as parents and teachers, who are responsible for their welfare and development.

## Procedures

Ellis (1977) has described an ABC(DE) model of emotional disturbance that illustrates how beliefs influence emotions and how people become upset. As shown in Figure 7.1, an individual's beliefs (B) about an activating event (A) cause his or her emotional and behavioral consequences (C). This explanation contrasts with the more commonly held view that emotions and behavior are caused

**Figure 7.1. Rational-Emotive Model of Emotions.**

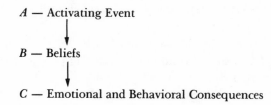

$A$ — Activating Event

$B$ — Beliefs

$C$ — Emotional and Behavioral Consequences

by events. Disputation (D), or questioning and challenging irrational beliefs that individuals may hold about themselves, others, and events, will lead to more constructive emotional and behavioral effects (E). *

Ellis and his colleagues have identified numerous irrational beliefs commonly held in our culture that appear to cause emotional disturbance. Some of the most frequently cited irrational beliefs and their rational alternatives are listed in Exhibit 7.1.

Ellis (1980, pp. 5–7) indicates that the irrational beliefs listed in Exhibit 7.1 and the numerous others that have been identified in the RET literature stem from the following three major irrational belief clusters:

1. "I must do well and win approval for my performance, or else I rate as a rotten person."
2. "Others must treat me considerately and kindly in precisely the way I want them to treat me; if they don't, society and the universe should severely blame, damn, and punish them for their inconsiderateness."
3. "Conditions under which I live must get arranged so that I get practically everything I want comfortably, quickly, and easily, and get virtually nothing that I don't want."

Bernard and Joyce (1984) state that these three irrational belief clusters cause major problems during childhood and adolescence as well as adulthood. Waters (1982, p. 572) has identified the following ten irrational beliefs of children.

1. "It's awful if others don't like me."
2. "I'm bad if I make a mistake."
3. "Everything should go my way; I should always get what I want."
4. "Things should come easy to me."
5. "The world should be fair and bad people must be punished."
6. "I shouldn't show my feelings."

**Exhibit 7.1. Common Irrational Beliefs and Their Rational Alternatives.**

---

1. The belief that you must feel loved or accepted by every significant person for almost everything you do, as opposed to the more realistic notion that approval of others is a desirable, but not a necessary goal, and that individuals should strive to do what they enjoy rather than what other people think they ought to do.

2. The belief that you should be thoroughly competent, adequate, and achieving in all possible respects if you are to consider yourself worthwhile, as opposed to realizing that everyone has limits, that you can try to do, or to do well, but that you will not be a worthless person if you do not achieve your goal, or be a better person if you do.

3. The idea that certain people are bad and should be punished, as opposed to the notion of accepting your own and others' misdeeds as errors to learn from and to try to correct in the future.

4. The idea that it is terrible, horrible, and awful when things do not go the way you want them to go, as opposed to the idea that if you are dissatisfied with a situation you should work to improve it rather than agonize over its imperfection.

5. The idea that human unhappiness is externally caused, as opposed to the idea that individuals create most of their own misery with their irrational thinking, and that individuals can minimize their unhappiness by changing their self-talk.

6. The idea that if something is or may be dangerous or fearsome, you should be terribly concerned and upset about it, as opposed to questioning the real dangers accompanying the event, determining the actual probabilities of their occurring or leading to dreadful consequences if they do occur, and realizing that worrying will not positively affect the situation.

7. The idea that it is easier to avoid than to face certain life difficulties and responsibilities, as opposed to realizing that meeting responsibilities is, in the long run, more rewarding.

8. The idea that an individual should be dependent on others and needs someone stronger to rely on, rather than accepting the fact that although others can help us, we are in some respects alone, and can be responsible for solving our own problems and making our own decisions.

9. The idea that one's past history is an all-important determiner of one's present behavior, and that because something once strongly affected one's life, it will indefinitely do so, as opposed to understanding that individuals can work to change their present thoughts and behaviors.

10. The idea that one should be very upset about other people's problems, as opposed to realizing that being upset will not help others to change.

11. The idea that there is a perfect solution to every problem, and that it is catastrophic if this perfect solution isn't found, as opposed to realizing that the best approach to a problem is to choose the most practical, feasible solution from among the available alternatives.

---

7.   "Adults should be perfect."
8.   "There's only one right answer."
9.   "I must win."
10.  "I shouldn't have to wait for anything."

In addition, Waters (1981, p. 6) identified ten irrational beliefs held by adolescents:

1.   "It would be awful if peers didn't like me. It would be awful to be a social loser."
2.   "I shouldn't make mistakes, especially social mistakes."
3.   "It's my parents' fault I'm so miserable."
4.   "I can't help it; that's just the way I am and I guess I'll always be this way."
5.   "The world should be fair and just."
6.   "It's awful when things do not go my way."
7.   "It's better to avoid challenges than to risk failure."
8.   "I must conform to my peers."
9.   "I can't stand to be criticized."
10.  "Others should always be responsible."

Waters (1981) has described seven goals of RET when used with young children. These include development of the following: (1) ability to identify emotions, (2) an emotional vocabulary, (3) ability to distinguish between helpful and hurtful feelings, (4) ability to differentiate between feelings and thoughts, (5) awareness of self-talk, (6) understanding of the relationship between self-talk and feelings, and (7) skill in making rational coping statements. With older children and adolescents, goals typically include development of skill in disputing irrational beliefs.

Many young children do not realize that a variety of feelings are possible and that a given feeling can vary in intensity. Bernard and Joyce (1984) advise therapists to use a number of exercises and games to begin increasing children's awareness and disclosure of feelings and thoughts. Suggestions include use of puppets, cartoon characters, and story-telling games as teaching devices. These allow the child to express thoughts and feelings while still maintaining a comfortable level of distance in his or her initial attempts to deal with a problem. During the initial stages of teaching the child to identify thoughts and feelings, the therapist or trainer may need to use a technique called labeling (Bernard & Joyce, 1984). When labeling is used, the practitioner provides tentative responses to questions directed to the child about thoughts and feelings, if the youngster cannot produce a spontaneous response. He or she is then asked to respond to the accuracy of the practitioner's hunches about these feelings and thoughts. The practitioner's statements about the child's probable feelings and thoughts frequently provide the impetus for the young client to elaborate on or correct those statements.

Once the child demonstrates emotional awareness, the practitioner typically begins to teach the ABC model of emotions. This is usually accomplished through presentation of numerous examples of how two people in the same situation may have different thoughts and therefore will have different feelings. For example, on the first day of school, some children may be happy, some may be scared, and some may be sad. These different feelings in response to the same situation are caused by different thoughts. A happy child may be thinking, "I can't wait to see all my friends again. I was getting bored at home." A child who is feeling scared may be thinking "I might not be able to do the work. What if that bully is in my class again?" The child who is feeling sad may be thinking "I'm really gonna miss all my friends from the beach. I'm probably gonna have a lot of trouble with the work again. This is gonna be miserable." It is frequently helpful to use a chart to teach the ABCs of emotions and to help the youngster identify a sequence of thoughts. An example of this type of chart can be seen in Exhibit 7.2.

Bernard and Joyce (1984, p. 195) recommend using the following types of prompts to elicit self-statements:

"What were you thinking when . . . happened?"
"What sorts of things were you saying to yourself when . . . ?"
"What name did you call your brother when he . . . ?"

### Exhibit 7.2. ABCs of Emotions.

---

*A—Activating Event*

I got my first math test of the year back and the grade was a D.

*B—Beliefs*

| *Irrational* | *Rational* |
|---|---|
| Oh no. This is terrible. | This is a really bad grade. |
| Everyone is probably laughing at me. | At least it's just the first exam. |
| I must be really stupid. | If I study more and ask for extra help, I can probably do better |
| I'll never be able to learn this stuff. | next time. |
| I'm just a failure. | It's just gonna be harder and take |
| I might as well give up. | more work than I thought. But I |
| Why should I bother with this stuff anyway? | need to do it, because I want a decent grade. |

*C—Emotional Consequence*

| | |
|---|---|
| Depressed | Concerned |

*Behavioral Consequence*

| | |
|---|---|
| Do nothing, Probably get another bad grade. | Ask for help. Study more. Probably get a better grade. |

---

"Tell me the first things which come into your mind when you think about . . . ?"

"Picture yourself back in class, what did you think when . . . ?"

Once the child or adolescent is able to identify feelings and precipitating thoughts, he or she can be taught the concepts of *rational* and *irrational*. With young children, the terms *helpful* and *hurtful* may be used instead. Bernard and Joyce (1984) define a rational thought as "a sensible and logical idea that seems to be true" and an irrational thought as "an unreasonable or absurd idea that seems to be false" (p. 225). They suggest that the child answer the following question to determine whether a thought is rational: "Is there enough evidence for me to say the thought is true?" Waters (1982, p. 576) suggests having children challenge their irrational beliefs by asking and answering the following questions.

1. "Is this belief based on fact, opinion, inference or assumption? Where is the evidence that this is really so?"
2. "Is it really awful? Is it true I couldn't stand it? Is it the worst that it could be?"
3. "Is this belief getting me what I want?"
4. "Why shouldn't it be so? Do I always have to get what I want?"
5. "Where is the evidence that this makes me worthless? How can this make me worthless or less than human?"

A number of methods have been used to help youngsters incorporate rational self-statements as part of their normal, natural approach to evaluating events. Rational self-instruction is one alternative. When this method is used, the practitioner draws up and models a set of rational self-statements for the child to rehearse and subsequently use in problem situations.

A second approach, empirical analysis, involves helping the child carry out an experiment to determine whether a belief is true. DiGiuseppe (1981, p. 64) described a case of a ten-year-old who had temper tantrums whenever his parents disagreed because he thought that such disagreements would lead to divorce.

"I asked Paul to set up an experiment to test his hypothesis that disagreement leads to divorce. He was willing to do so and we designed a questionnaire for this purpose. Paul polled his teacher and principal, several store-keepers, a police officer, and others about whether they decided to divorce every time they argued with their spouses. Paul found that disagreements were common in marriage and rarely resulted in divorce. His symptoms ceased."

Disputation, or challenging, is the most frequently used method of changing irrational thinking. Through disputation, the youngster is taught how to challenge irrational beliefs and to generate alternative rational thoughts. Through discussion and exercises, the practitioner addresses each of the irrational beliefs held by the child or adolescent, pointing out why the beliefs do not make sense and suggesting more rational alternatives.

A final approach, rational-emotive imagery (Maultsby,

1975), involves having the child relax and then rehearse rational thinking through imagery. The child is asked to imagine the problem situation and to imagine himself or herself thinking rational thoughts and behaving in an appropriate constructive manner.

As indicated previously, the rational-emotive approach is frequently used in classroom preventive programs called rational-emotive education (REE). The goal of REE is to teach the basic principles of rational thinking and the basic methods of using the rational-emotive approach to address daily stressors. Students are taught that their thoughts cause their feelings and that they can change their feelings by changing the way they think. Major irrational beliefs and their rational alternatives are also covered.

Knaus's (1974) REE manual describes classroom activities that focus on five major topics: (1) understanding feelings and where they come from; (2) challenging irrational beliefs; (3) challenging feelings of inferiority; (4) learning, mistake-making, and imperfection; and (5) demanding, catastrophizing, and challenging. Bernard and Joyce (1984) outline REE sessions for young children (five to seven years), older children (eight to twelve years) and adolescents (thirteen to seventeen years). The program for younger children focuses on understanding feelings and the relationship of thoughts and feelings. Rational self-statements are also taught. The programs for older children and adolescents include disputation of irrational beliefs.

### Specialized Assessment Instruments

A few scales have been developed with the specific purpose of identifying irrational beliefs in children and adolescents. It is generally suggested, however, that the practitioner engage in a thorough multidimensional assessment of behavior and cognitions when doing an assessment for intervention planning.

The Children's Survey of Rational Beliefs (Knaus, 1974) has one form for children aged seven to ten and another for those aged ten to thirteen. The eighteen items in the form for younger children and the thirty-eight items in the form for older children are in multiple choice format and assess the presence of a variety of irrational beliefs. Unfortunately, no normative, reliability, or validity data are available for this scale.

The Idea Inventory (Kassinove, Crisci, & Tiegerman, 1977) is appropriate for students in grades 4 through 12; it also assesses the presence of irrational beliefs, using thirty-three items for which the student indicates agreement or disagreement. This scale has been found to correlate moderately with other personality scales measuring disturbance.

The Child and Adolescent Scale of Irrationality (Bernard & Laws, 1988) is a recently developed instrument that consists of forty-four items for which the child or adolescent indicates extent of agreement. This instrument has six subscales derived through factor analysis: Self-Downing, Nonconformity, Demands on Others, Dependence, Low Frustration Tolerance, and Demands for Comfort. Initial studies with this scale show a reasonable degree of internal consistency and a relationship with other measures of emotional problems.

## Review of Research

Published research concerning the efficacy of the rational-emotive approach with children and adolescents is very limited, although a number of doctoral dissertations have addressed its effectiveness. Studies have been conducted to examine its effects on normal students (DiGuiseppe & Kassinove, 1976), those with high levels of anxiety (Smith, 1979; Warren, Deffenbacher, & Brading, 1976), those with low self-esteem (Bernard, 1979), and those with learning disabilities (Staggs, 1979). The rational-emotive approach has also been used with disruptive high school students (Block, 1978) and those categorized as emotionally disturbed (Patton, 1985). Most of the research has indicated that irrational beliefs decrease in children and adolescents as a result of rational-emotive therapy or its classroom counterpart, rational-emotive education. A smaller percentage of studies has shown changes in anxiety, self-esteem, or behavior.

In a review of the literature, Hajzler and Bernard (1991) examined forty-six studies that focused on use of RET with school-aged children. All compared the use of RET with a no-treatment control group. In 92 percent of the studies the authors found that RET reduced irrationality; 64 percent showed effects on behavior and 50 percent showed effects on anxiety. However, there was no evidence that changes in emotions or behavior were brought about by or correlated with changes in irrational beliefs.

Hajzler and Bernard (1991) indicate that duration of treatment is an important factor in predicting effectiveness. They recommend that the rational-emotive intervention extend the equivalent of fifteen sessions at minimum, each lasting fifty minutes. In addition, they suggest that use of a variety of rehearsal methods including homework assignments, behavioral rehearsal, and rational-emotive imagery can enhance effectiveness. In a final recommendation, they address the issue of practitioner training, pointing out that extensive training is needed in order to implement rational-emotive education programs properly and to conduct rational-emotive therapy. They also contend that the lack of emotional and behavioral change in some subjects participating in effectiveness studies may have been the result of inadequate practitioner training.

## Summary

The rational-emotive approach to helping children and adolescents develop coping skills is well suited for use in the school setting, partially because of its extensive didactic component. This approach focuses on eliminating irrational beliefs and teaching rational thinking. In addition to its use in individual and group counseling, rational-emotive concepts can be taught through preventive education programs implemented with entire classrooms. Parents are also frequently involved in rational-emotive counseling, as they are considered essential adjuncts in helping children change their patterns of thinking, feeling, and behaving (Joyce, 1990).

Based on numerous years of clinical experience, Bernard (1990) has set forth twelve guidelines for using RET with school-aged children. These include the following:

1. Use as many "concrete" teaching aids as possible.
2. Work on one emotional/behavioral problem at a time.
3. For children older than seven, illustrate the relationship

among activating events, thoughts, feelings, and behavior with diagrams.

4. Assess the student for multiple errors in thinking.
5. Allow the student to dispute his or her own errors in thinking before you do.
6. When disputing thoughts, tie the thoughts and their disputes to specific situations experienced by the student.
7. Make sure that students who are older than seven can explain the relationship between changes in thinking and changes in feeling.
8. To maintain student interest, be animated when disputing.
9. Repeat disputational arguments if the student appears to continue believing an irrational idea.
10. Discuss how the student can cope with the problem in the future using the rational-emotive approach.
11. Use the following process to help students internalize the rational-thinking approach for use in specific situations: (a) role-play with modeling of rational self-statements by the trainer, (b) overt rehearsal of rational self-statements by the student, (c) covert rehearsal of rational self-statements, (d) rehearsal of appropriate behavior in the problem situation through role-play.
12. Assign homework involving use of new skills between sessions.

A large body of literature exists regarding the practice of RET, and a number of studies have begun to establish the effectiveness of this approach with children and adolescents. Proponents of the rational-emotive approach with school-aged populations now face the challenge of increasing the research literature in this area in order to provide additional evidence of effectiveness and direction for practitioners regarding use of specific therapeutic components and implementation procedures.

*Eight*

# Developing
# Stress-Reducing Thought Patterns

Stress inoculation training is a structured approach to helping individuals learn to deal with stressful situations through use of cognitive-behavioral procedures. This approach was developed by Donald Meichenbaum, and although to date most evaluative studies have been conducted with adult populations, the approach appears to hold promise for those working with older children and adolescents. Stress inoculation training is based on the transactional model of stress (Lazarus & Folkman, 1984) discussed in Chapter One. This model describes stress as a process consisting of a stimulus, individual characteristics, and the stress reaction of the individual. The manner in which individuals appraise stressful events and their coping resources is seen as a particularly important determinant of the stress reaction. Stress inoculation training can help individuals understand the nature of stress, enhance their appraisal and coping skills, and, thereby, decrease negative, unconstructive stress reactions.

## Development

In an early comprehensive work on cognitive-behavior modification, Donald Meichenbaum (1977) explained the process of stress inoculation training, a procedure first described in an unpublished manuscript by Meichenbaum and Cameron (1972) delineating a training procedure for dealing with anxiety. A few years later, reports appeared in the literature concerning uses of this approach with adults to deal with anger (Novaco, 1977) and pain (Turk, 1975).

Meichenbaum's (1977) description of stress inoculation training emphasized the idea that it is a coping skills approach to treatment that can give clients a set of coping responses to use across a variety of stress-producing situations. In describing the development of this approach, Meichenbaum (1977) cited other investigators who were working at the same time and developing similar approaches. These included Goldfried and his colleagues (Goldfried, Decenteceo, & Weinberg, 1974), who developed a treatment approach called systematic rational restructuring, which combines rational-emotive therapy and behavioral procedures, and Suinn and Richardson (1971), who developed an approach called anxiety management training. Meichenbaum (1977) pointed out that these approaches have a number of common components: (1) teaching clients the role of cognitions in contributing to their problem; (2) training in identification of self-statements and images and in self-monitoring of problem behavior; (3) training in problem-solving procedures; (4) modeling of self-statements and images; (5) modeling, rehearsal, and encouragement of positive self-evaluation, attention focusing, and other coping skills; (6) using behavior therapy procedures such as relaxation training, coping imagery training, and behavioral rehearsal; and (7) assigning behavioral homework tasks.

In his 1977 book, Meichenbaum cites the work of Epstein (1967) and Orne (1965) on stress and anxiety as contributing to the theoretical framework and development of stress inoculation training. Both of these authors emphasize the importance of paced mastery experiences in helping individuals learn to cope with stress. Orne (1965, p. 315) states, "One way of enabling an individual to become resistant to a stress is to allow him to have appropriate prior experience with the stimulus involved. The biological notion of immunization provides such a model. If an individual is given the opportunity to deal with a stimulus that is mildly stressful and he is able to do so successfully (mastering it in a psychological sense) he will tend to be able to tolerate a similar stimulus of somewhat greater intensity in the future." Orne further contends, "It would seem that one can markedly affect an individual's tolerance of stress by manipulating his beliefs about his performance in the situation . . . and his feeling that he can control his own behavior" (1965, p. 316).

### Procedures

Meichenbaum (1985) indicates that stress inoculation training typically consists of three phases: (1) an education or conceptualization phase, (2) a skills acquisition phase, and (3) an application and follow-through phase. The specific content of each phase varies with the type of problem being addressed.

The conceptualization phase focuses on establishing a positive, collaborative relationship between the trainer and trainee and helping the trainee understand the nature of stress in terms of the transactional model discussed previously. Meichenbaum (1985, p. 27) outlines the following objectives of this phase:

1.  Establish a collaborative relationship with the client and with significant others where appropriate,
2.  Discuss the client's stress-related problems and symptoms, focusing on a situational analysis,
3.  Collect information in the form of interviews, questionnaires, self-monitoring procedures, imagery-based techniques, and behavioral assessments,
4.  Assess the client's expectations with regard to effectiveness of the training program and formulate treatment plans, establishing short, intermediate, and long-term goals,
5.  Educate the client about the transactional nature of stress and coping and consider the role that cognitions and emotions play in engendering and maintaining stress,
6.  Offer a conceptual model or reconceptualization of the client's stress reactions,

7.  Anticipate and subsume possible client resistance and reasons for treatment nonadherence.

Thus, this initial phase emphasizes establishment of the client-trainer relationship, description of the nature of stress, and collection of information that will help in formulation of a specific training plan. Meichenbaum states that during the conceptualization phase, the trainee should be encouraged to view stressful situations as "problems-to-be-solved" as opposed to personal threats. The three-stage conceptual model of stress that is presented, which explains stress in terms of a stressor, intervening individual characteristics, and a stress reaction, emphasizes the contribution of an individual's reactions to the stress he or she experiences. When people understand that their reactions contribute to stress, the knowledge helps them see that individuals can control and change their stress reactions.

Other information conveyed during this stage includes an explanation of the phases of cognitive activity an individual goes through in reacting to a stressor: preparing for the stressor, confronting and trying to handle the stressful event, coping with feelings of being overwhelmed, and reflecting about coping efforts. The explanations of the stress process and phases of cognitive activity are based on and include examples of the specific type of problem the client is experiencing.

The skills acquisition phase focuses on helping the trainee build a repertoire of effective coping responses. The specific skills taught during this phase vary with the needs of the trainees and the particular stress-related problem being addressed. These coping skills include those that are problem focused, such as problem-solving skills and social skills, and those that are emotion regulating, such as relaxation skills and cognitive coping skills. According to published reports of the use of stress inoculation training, relaxation skills and cognitive coping skills appear to be the ones most often taught.

Meichenbaum (1985) suggests that the introduction of relaxation should be linked to the explanation of stress provided during the conceptualization phase. In this manner, relaxation can be described as a coping skill, which can be used in response to various stressors in order to alleviate or decrease negative stress reactions. Relaxation is typically presented in the manner described in Chapter Two, as an active coping skill that requires practice. A variety of relaxation procedures, as indicated in Chapter Two, may be taught. In addition, it is important to discuss the specific situations and manner in which the trainee might use these procedures in the future as a means of reducing negative stress reactions.

Meichenbaum (1985) indicates that a variety of cognitive procedures may be employed in stress inoculation training. These include cognitive restructuring, problem solving, and guided self-dialogue.

Cognitive restructuring is based on Aaron Beck's (1976) work on cognitive therapy. The first step in cognitive restructuring is to help clients become aware of their thoughts and feelings and to realize that these thoughts may not be facts. Meichenbaum (1985, p. 60) suggests using the following questions to help the trainee identify thoughts.

> What thoughts were running through your head just before you came in to see me? Do you have similar thoughts and feelings in stressful situations at home? What do you think will happen in such situations? What do you picture happening? What are you saying to yourself in that situation? Then what? How do you know that that will indeed happen? What is the evidence of a threat? How serious is it? What coping resources are available?

After noting the thoughts typically generated by the trainees, the trainer assists them in evaluating these thoughts logically. This can be done through discussion similar to that described in the chapter on rational-emotive therapy. The discussion can be supplemented by requesting that the trainees carry out personal experiments to validate their expectations and beliefs. For example, through a personal experiment, trainees may be asked to test their expectations concerning how others might react to a specific behavior. The trainees may believe that others think they are stupid and will laugh at anything they say. To test the validity of this belief, trainees might be asked, as a homework assignment, to volunteer to answer a question in class and observe the subsequent behavior of other students.

Problem solving is addressed in the manner described in Chapter Three. Meichenbaum (1985, p. 67) enumerates a number of steps that are common to problem-solving training programs focusing on improving coping skills. These include the following:

1. Define the stressor or stress reactions as a problem-to-be-solved,
2. Set realistic goals as concretely as possible by stating the problem in behavioral terms and by delineating steps necessary to reach each goal,
3. Generate a wide range of possible alternative courses of action,
4. Imagine and consider how others might respond if asked to deal with a similar stress problem,
5. Evaluate the pros and cons of each proposed solution and rank order the solutions from least to most practical and desirable,
6. Rehearse strategies and behaviors by means of imagery, behavioral rehearsal, and graduated practice,
7. Try out the most acceptable and feasible solution,
8. Expect some failures, but reward self for having tried,
9. Reconsider the original problem in light of the attempt at problem solving.

Guided self-dialogue is similar to the self-instruction training procedures that are described in Chapter Six. This coping skill helps trainees to do the following:

1. assess the demands of a situation and plan for future stressors,
2. control negative self-defeating, stress-engendering thoughts, images, and feelings,

3.  acknowledge, use, and relabel the arousal experienced,

4.  cope with intense dysfunctional emotions that might be experienced,

5.  'psych' themselves up to confront stressful situations, and

6.  reflect on their performance and reinforce themselves for having attempted to cope [Meichenbaum, 1985, p. 70].

As described in Chapter Six the trainer helps the trainees develop a series of coping self-statements that assist them in preparing for the stressor, confronting the stressor, coping with feelings of being overwhelmed, evaluating coping efforts, and rewarding themselves for success. Exhibit 8.1 presents an example of appropriate self-statements that could be made during these phases by a child who overreacts to corrective feedback (Cartledge & Milburn, 1980).

The objective of the application and follow-through phase is to encourage trainees to implement the newly learned coping skills in day-to-day situations and to incorporate them as part of the trainees' behavioral repertoire. This can be done through a variety of rehearsal techniques including imagery rehearsal, behavioral rehearsal, role-playing, modeling, and graduated in vivo practice (Meichenbaum, 1985).

In imagery rehearsal the trainee, while relaxed, imagines coping with progressively more stressful situations. Behavioral rehearsal, role-playing, and modeling can be implemented as described in Chapter Four. In addition, Meichenbaum (1985) suggests use of a role reversal type of role-play in which the trainee plays the trainer and the trainer assumes the role of novice trainee. In addition to providing an opportunity for rehearsal for the trainee, this technique also affords a good opportunity for the trainer to assess the trainee's level of understanding of the training procedures. Graduated in vivo practice is an essential component of stress inoculation training. It is accomplished through homework assignments in which the trainee is instructed to use specific skills in specific types of situations. These assignments gradually increase in difficulty throughout the training.

### Exhibit 8.1. Self-Statements from Stress Inoculation Training for Problems with Response to Corrective Feedback.

*Preparation for Provocation*

If the teacher marks something wrong I can handle it.
I know what to do if I get upset.
Making a mistake is not so bad.

*Impact on Confrontation*

Keep calm.
Think about the ones you got correct.
It's silly to get angry about one problem.
The teacher is really right to show me what I did wrong.
Being corrected helps me learn.

*Coping with Arousal*

I'm beginning to breathe hard; relax.
Stop and think about all the good work you did today.
Try to keep cool.

*Reflection on Provocation*

a. When conflict is unresolved:
   It partly worked.
   I can do better next time.
   This is hard to do but I'll keep trying.
b. When conflict is resolved or coping is successful:
   I did a good job that time; I even smiled at the teacher.
   I can be a good student. The teacher likes me.

*Source:* From G. Cartledge and J. F. Milburn, *Teaching Social Skills to Children.* Copyright year date © 1980. Reprinted with permission of Allyn and Bacon.

Meichenbaum (1985) discusses the special role of relapse prevention in stress inoculation training. Through relapse prevention, trainees are helped to develop coping responses to situations in which they may fail to use appropriate coping strategies. They are helped to anticipate failures and setbacks and to deal with these situations constructively. For example, an adolescent who is participating in stress inoculation training because of anger control problems may lose his temper in an interaction with his teacher. During training, he can be taught to anticipate this occurrence and to view it as one mistake that will not necessarily be repeated if he keeps working at implementing anger control strategies.

Follow-through in stress inoculation training is accomplished through fading of training sessions and scheduling of booster sessions. During the last phase of training, sessions may be scheduled every two weeks instead of every week. Booster sessions may be scheduled at one-, three-, six-, and twelve-month intervals. This schedule provides an opportunity for the trainee to use newly learned strategies with some trainer support and for the trainer to deal with any specific difficult situations that may arise.

### Specialized Assessment Techniques

A variety of behavioral assessment techniques can be used during the conceptualization phase of stress inoculation training. These include traditional behavioral assessment techniques such as interviewing, self-monitoring, observation, and self-report questionnaires. Meichenbaum (1985) describes an assessment procedure called imagery-based recall that can be useful in helping trainees become aware of various aspects of their stress response. Using this procedure, trainees are asked to close their eyes, relax, and imagine or relive various stress experiences. They are then asked to describe anything they remember noticing, thinking, feeling, or doing, and the impact that these thoughts, feelings, and behaviors had on their stress level. After using this procedure to obtain descriptions of a number of stress-related situations, the trainer can develop hypotheses concerning cross-situational issues that need to be addressed during training.

### Review of Research

The effectiveness of stress inoculation training has been studied with a variety of adult populations. It has been used in medical settings to help patients deal with a range of medical problems such as chronic pain, headaches, arthritis, and burns (Turk, Meichenbaum, & Genest, 1983). An additional use in medical settings has been to prepare patients for surgery and medical and dental examinations. Melamed and Siegel (1975) conducted one of the few studies of stress inoculation training for children with medical problems. In this investigation, hospitalized children who viewed a film showing a peer coping with surgery had better preoperative and postoperative adjustment than did control group children.

Stress inoculation has also been used to help various occupational groups deal with job-related stress. Of particular interest to those who work with children and adolescents in school settings are studies that show stress inoculation training to be an effective means of helping teachers deal with school-related stress. Forman and her colleagues (Cecil & Forman, 1990; Forman, 1982, 1983; Sharp & Forman, 1985) have reported on a number of investigations in which public school teachers showed reduced levels of stress after they received stress inoculation training that included instruction in relaxation and rational restructuring. The interventions helped teachers reduce their own stress as well as become "coping models" for their students.

Another major application of stress inoculation training that has received some attention in the child and adolescent literature is use with anger control problems. McCullough, Huntsinger, and May (1977) presented a case study of an effective anger control intervention with acting-out adolescents using a stress inoculation training approach. Schlichter and Horan (1981) described a stress inoculation training approach to treating anger problems of institutionalized delinquents.

In a school-based intervention study, Feindler, Marriott, and Iwata (1984) examined the effectiveness of anger control training with junior high school students in a program for multisuspended delinquents. The treatment program for the students in this study was conducted over ten sessions and included training in analyzing the components of the provocation cycle (antecedent anger cues, aggressive responses, and consequent events) through self-monitoring. This was followed by instruction in two time-out responses: (1) inserting a time delay between the provoking stimulus and the automatic response and (2) ignoring the provoking stimulus for a few seconds. Students also received instruction in relaxation, assertive responses, and problem solving. In addition, they were instructed in cognitive control techniques. These included self-instruction, modification of interpretations of aggression-eliciting situations, self-evaluation of performance during a conflict situation, and "thinking ahead" through anticipation of future consequences. Exhibit 8.2 summarizes the strategies taught during this training program.

**Exhibit 8.2. Summary of Anger Control Procedures for Use with Aggressive Adolescents.**

I. Assessment and Analysis of Provocation Cues and Anger Responses: Self-Monitoring Techniques
    1. Identification of aggressive responses to provocation, antecedent-provoking stimuli, and consequent events
    2. Self-rating of anger components
    3. Training in self-recording and compilation of own data
    4. Analysis of provocation sequences and behavioral patterns
II. Training of Alternative Responses to External Provoking Stimuli
    A. Self-instructions
        1. Definition and generation of relevant self-instructions (termed REMINDERS)
        2. Modeling and role-playing of *how* and *when* to use self-verbalizations to guide overt and covert behavior
        3. Training in both generalized and specific self-instructions
    B. Self-evaluation skills
        1. Determination of individual self-evaluative statements that currently function as reinforcers or punishers
        2. Definition of self-evaluations as a form of self-instruction that provides feedback and guides performance in both re-solved and unresolved provocation incidents
    C. Thinking-ahead techniques
        1. Presentation of problem-solving strategy designed to help client use the estimation of future negative consequences for misbehavior to guide current responses to provocation
        2. Modeling and role-playing of *how* and *when* to use self-generated contingency statements concerning negative consequences
    D. Relaxation techniques
        1. Presentation of arousal management techniques to aid in the identification of physiological responses to provocation and to control muscle tension during or in anticipation of conflicts
        2. Deep breathing as a time delay and an alternative response
        3. Deep muscle relaxation training
III. Techniques to Control Own Provocation Behaviors
    E. Angry behavior cycle
        1. Discrimination of own behaviors that may act as provocation cues to others and of escalating sequences of aggression
        2. Contracting for change in frequency and/or intensity of nonverbal (voice volume, tone, threatening gestures) and/or verbal (threats, teases, arguments) aggressive behaviors that may provoke others
    F. Assertion without aggression
        1. Examination of peer pressure, conformity and conflict with authority issues

**Exhibit 8.2. Summary of Anger Control Procedures for Use with Aggressive Adolescents, Cont'd.**

2. Enumeration of personal rights and responsibilities
3. Modeling and role-playing of assertion techniques including empathetic assertion, fogging, broken record, confrontation, minimal assertive response

*Source:* Feindler, E. L., Marriott, S. A., & Iwata, M. (1984). Group anger control training for junior high school delinquents. *Cognitive Therapy and Research, 8,* 304.

Training was accomplished through the following sequence. The trainer presented the technique in a didactic manner and modeled its use. Students then rehearsed use of the technique with a conflict incident gained from self-monitoring information. Students also rehearsed use of the technique with graduated presentations of specific provocations. Homework assignments provided additional opportunities for rehearsal. Results of the study, which compared treated students with a no-treatment control condition, yielded support for the use of the procedures described above. The anger control training had greatest impact on low-frequency, high-severity aggressive behaviors.

Other studies documenting the effectiveness of this type of training with aggressive children have been reported by Lochman and his colleagues (Lochman, Burch, Curry, & Lampron, 1984; Lochman, Nelson, & Sims, 1981). The training program examined in these studies consisted of twelve small group sessions held twice weekly and lasting forty minutes each. Training topics included exploration of reactions to peers, identification of anger-arousing situations, social problem solving, physiological awareness, and use of positive self-statements and self-instructions. The training program, which included various role-play and rehearsal activities, resulted in decreases in the children's aggressive and disruptive behavior.

Stress inoculation training has also been used as an intervention for dealing with anxiety. Stevens and Pihl (1983) explored the use of this procedure with seventh-grade students who reacted adversely to test situations. Training took place over ten daily sessions of forty-five minutes each and included instruction in how to use self-instructions and problem solving as well as rehearsal, modeling, and role-playing. The training resulted in improvements in coping ability.

## Summary

Stress inoculation training helps individuals learn to cope with potentially stressful situations through provision of information on the nature of stress, skills training, and application opportunities. Although a relatively small amount of research has been conducted on the effectiveness of stress inoculation training with school-aged populations, this approach appears to have good potential for effectiveness in dealing with anger and anxiety problems of adolescents. The small number of studies that have been completed with adolescents has yielded positive results. The adult literature indicates that downward extension of the age of trainees, to include adolescents, will likely yield positive outcomes if the trainees have the cognitive ability to deal with the conceptual material that is presented as part of the training.

Stress inoculation training combines most of the procedures described in previous chapters and emphasizes the importance of helping the trainees understand their own behavior, the stress process, and how the various coping strategies work to alleviate negative stress reactions and problematic behavior. Such training appears to have great potential for helping trainees develop a broad repertoire of coping strategies and thereby having the potential to deal independently with a wide range of potentially problematic situations after training is terminated, and to do so effectively.

*Nine*

# Changing Beliefs
# About Success and Failure

The beliefs of children and adolescents about their successes and failures are significant contributors to future successes and failures. A number of studies have shown that beliefs concerning causality influence future expectations, affect, persistence, and performance (Harvey, Ickes, & Kidd, 1978).

Attribution retraining is a cognitive-behavioral intervention that focuses on the development of beliefs about the causes of success and failure that will have a constructive effect on future behavior and goal attainment. Weiner (1972, 1979) found that when asked to identify the reason for success or failure on a task as well as factors that would lead to success or failure in the future, individuals named four major causes: (1) their ability, (2) their effort or motivation, (3) the ease or difficulty of the task, or (4) luck. These four causes explain success and failure according to two dimensions: internal versus external cause and stable versus variable situation. Ability and effort are internal, while task difficulty and luck are external. Ability and task difficulty are stable, while effort and luck are variable. Attribution retraining attempts to increase the

success of children and adolescents in coping with academic and
social tasks through instruction and feedback regarding causal
beliefs.

## Development

Attribution retraining has its roots in the social psychology literature and the literature on attribution theory, which examines and
attempts to explain the causes that individuals attribute to events
they perceive. In 1958 Fritz Heider published *The Psychology of
Interpersonal Relations* in which he indicated that a major task of
an individual in understanding the social and physical world was
to find the underlying causes of things that he or she perceived.
Heider divided causal explanations of events into two types: those
with personal causes and those with environmental causes. He indicated that people explain an event by either attributing its cause
to the person involved with it or by attributing its cause to some
external source. In response to this notion, social psychologists engaged in numerous studies that described how individuals searched
for and explained the causes of social behavior. In the late 1960s and
early 1970s researchers began to write about "attribution therapy,"
a procedure through which it was thought debilitating effects of
psychological symptoms could be reduced by teaching new attributions for those symptoms (Nisbett & Schachter, 1966; Ross, Rodin,
& Zimbardo, 1969; Valins & Nisbett, 1971).

The literature regarding attribution retraining as it applies
to children and adolescents began to develop in the early and mid-
1970s. An early report described a program called personal causation training (DeCharms, 1972). This program was implemented by
classroom teachers with inner-city sixth and seventh graders and
consisted of exercises that taught students to assume personal responsibility for their classroom successes and failures by viewing
themselves as the "origins" rather than the "pawns" of their behavior. Students who participated in this training were found to have
higher achievement levels than students who did not participate.

In 1975, Carol Dweck published an important initial study
of the effects of attribution retraining on children. The study attempted to determine whether altering children's perceptions of the
relationships between their behavior and their failure would lead to

a change in maladaptive responses to failure. Dweck hypothesized that training that taught the child to take responsibility for failure and to attribute it to insufficient effort would lead to increased persistence in the face of failure. Subjects in this study were twelve children, ranging in age from eight to thirteen, who had been identified by school personnel as exhibiting behavioral characteristics of learned helplessness (children who expected failure and were debilitated by it).

The children were divided into two groups; each group participated in twenty-five daily sessions of training. During each session, the children earned a token if they correctly solved a specified number of arithmetic problems within a specified time period. In the Success Only group the children were given sets of problems that were within their ability range. Failures were ignored and successes were reinforced. In the Attribution Retraining group, 20 percent of the sets of problems given were beyond the ability range of the children and thus likely to result in failure. On every failure, however, the children were given an effort attribution for their failure, with the experimenter remarking, "That means you should have tried harder."

After this training children in both groups were presented with difficult puzzles that were likely to result in failure, and their persistence was measured. While the Success Only group exhibited performance deficits in the face of failure, the Attribution Retraining group did not. Dweck concluded that children who believe failure to be a result of lack of motivation are likely to escalate their efforts in attempts to reach a goal, and that this type of attribution can be trained.

A number of studies followed Dweck's (1975) study with "learned helpless" children. Most of the literature in this area has focused on low-achieving students, including hyperactive students and those with learning disabilities. A second area of focus for attribution retraining has been depressed children and adolescents.

### Procedures

Beck, Rush, Shaw, and Emery (1979) describe a basic cognitive therapy process that can be adapted for use in attribution retraining with children and adolescents. The process involves five steps:

1.  Instruct the individual about the relationship between thoughts, motivation, emotion, and behavior.
2.  Introduce the concept of explanatory (attributional) style and the idea that it occurs automatically.
3.  Train the individual to interrupt the automatic process of providing self-defeating explanations for negative events.
4.  Train the individual to test an explanation against the facts of the situation when possible.
5.  Train the individual to substitute a positive interpretation of an event when testing an explanation against facts is not possible.

Cecil and Medway (1986) indicate that attribution retraining with low-achieving students who have motivational problems can be easily implemented by school personnel using training procedures similar to those suggested for self-instructional training (see Chapter Six). The authors state that the classroom teacher can model effort attributions for students and then provide reinforcement when these statements are made during schoolwork. They believe that instances of effort should be reinforced even if the student is not entirely successful, and that if criticism is given, it should be specific to the task and should be given only for tasks on which the teacher thinks the student has not put forth effort. They further contend that attribution retraining is most likely to be effective if classroom teachers incorporate it into their daily classroom behaviors.

Peterson (1992) provides some examples of how this incorporation might be done by linking feedback on performance with helpful attributions. He indicates that criticism should consist of specific explanations, such as "You didn't spend enough time on that math problem," and praise should contain very general attributions, such as "You are a very conscientious individual."

Thomas (1989) describes a three-step sequence of activities that can be used by classroom teachers in attribution retraining:

1. Students should be helped to become aware of their self-talk (inner dialogue) by teacher modeling of self-talk during problem-solving tasks. This should be done as a means of demonstrating both positive and negative attributions. In addition, group

discussions should be used to identify self-statements that help and hinder persistence and positive self-evaluation.

2. Once students are able to distinguish between mastery-oriented and helpless self-statements, they will need to practice positive attributional statements in order to use them fluently. Students can practice with a variety of problem-solving tasks during which they should be encouraged to talk to themselves aloud using statements that attribute outcome to effort and that are self-encouraging. Problem-solving tasks should be moderate in difficulty and should present opportunities for both success and failure.

3. After practice sessions as described above, practice should be incorporated into class sessions in a variety of subjects where new concepts and skills are learned. Students might be encouraged to keep diaries that note areas of difficulty and describe their progress in using positive attributional statements.

Borkowski, Weyhing, and Turner (1986, pp. 133–134) provide an example of a trainer explaining and modeling use of positive attributions for a student during a study in which the effects of self-instruction training and attribution retraining were assessed.

> I made a mistake on this sheet. Can you tell me why I made the mistake? We all make mistakes and there are a lot of reasons "why." What are some of the reasons you may make mistakes in school?
>
> Here, looking at these pictures will help us talk about it. (The experimenter shows the cartoon pictures of four frowning children with "I didn't try to use the self-control steps," "I am unlucky," "the teacher doesn't like me" and "the task was too hard.") I sometimes think that I make an error because I am unlucky. Sometimes I think it is because the task is too hard. When I think these things I get discouraged because I don't have control over luck or the task. When I think that I goofed because I am dumb, then I really feel like a loser and don't want to try at all.
>
> However, I usually find that it wasn't any of these reasons that caused the problem. The problem is usually

that I did not try to use the self-control steps. This is important because unlike the other reasons (point to the pictures labeled "teacher doesn't like me," "unlucky," "task is too hard"), I have control over this one (point to picture labeled "I didn't try to use the self-control steps"). See, this is the usual reason why I failed (point to the picture labeled "I didn't try to use the self-control steps"), and not these reasons (point to the other pictures).

Let's see, here is the problem that I failed. I need to redo the problem and this time try to use the self-control steps. Here goes. . . . (The instructor goes through the self-control steps.)

Okay, this time I got it right. Why do you think that I got it right? Which of these pictures expresses why I got it right? (The instructor shows the four pictures of smiling children labeled "I tried and used the self-control steps," "the teacher likes me," "I am lucky," "the task was easy.") All of these pictures show why people think that they get things correct. Why do you think that you get things right in school?

This is the usual reason right here. (Point to the picture labeled "I tried hard and used the self-control steps.") It is the most important reason because I have control over myself.

Fowler and Peterson (1981) describe an attribution retraining procedure that includes modeling, overt rehearsal, and covert rehearsal. Children first listened to a recording of a child who modeled effort attributions such as "No, I didn't get that. That means I have to try hard." They were then asked to put these statements in their own words and practice saying them aloud. After saying them aloud, they practiced saying them in a whisper, and then covertly. They subsequently worked on problem-solving tasks and were reminded to "tell yourself what you say" when they encountered success and failure.

In addition to its use as a method of building coping skills of low-achieving students, attribution retraining has been used to

assist depressed children and adolescents to develop more constructive responses to events. Rehm (1977) contended that a maladaptive
attributional style was one cause of symptoms of depression. Depressed youngsters tend to make internal, stable, and global attributions for negative events, and external, unstable, and specific
attributions for positive events (Abramson, Seligman, & Teasdale,
1978). When something negative happens to depressed youngsters,
they blame themselves, think that the negative event or situation
will continue to occur, and that it will have a broad influence on
them. When a positive event or situation occurs, they think it was
the result of external causes, is unlikely to occur again, and has
limited significance.

Stark, Reynolds, and Kaslow (1987) indicated that a multicomponent cognitive-behavioral treatment program that included
reattribution training could be effective in treating depressed children. This training focused on teaching the child to attribute failure
to external, unstable, and specific causes, and success to internal,
stable, and global causes when it is realistic to do so.

Such training can be accomplished through didactic instruction, coaching, and rehearsal. Youngsters can be taught the meaning and importance of attributions, the major types of attributions,
and the effects that attributions have on depressed individuals.
Problem situations that reflect situations typically faced by youngsters can be used to provide opportunities for coaching and practice
in use of adaptive causal attributions. Exhibit 9.1 provides an outline of the content of attribution retraining for depressed
youngsters.

### Specialized Assessment Instruments

The most frequently used attribution measure is the Intellectual
Achievement Responsibility (IAR) Scale (Crandall, Katkovsky, &
Crandall, 1965). This scale was designed to assess the degree to
which children believe the intellectual failures and successes they
experience are a result of their own behavior or the behavior of
important others in their environment such as teachers, parents, or
friends. The scale has thirty-four items that depict positive or neg-

**Exhibit 9.1. Outline of Attribution Retraining.**

---

*Introduction to attribution concepts*

   Therapists teach the meaning of consequences (positive and negative) of events.
   Therapists teach the meaning of causes of events (ability, effort, luck, other people/things).
   Therapists demonstrate how thoughts about consequences and causes affect our feelings about meanings of events.
   Given hypothetical situations, children indicate how they would think about the causes and consequences if they happened to them.

*Application of attribution training*

   Therapists describe typical ways that unhappy persons think about consequences and causes of events.
   Children complete homework of choosing three events and writing down positive consequences and causes of these events.

*Implementation of attribution retraining*

   Review homework.
   Extend examples of how children who are unhappy think about events.
   Given hypothetical situations, children in a group generate realistic, adaptive attributions.
   Coaching and modeling are used to facilitate discussion of alternative attributions.

---

*Source:* Stark, Brookman, & Frazier, 1990, p. 122.

ative achievement situations and present two alternative attributions: an internal attribution in which responsibility for the outcome of the situation is related to the individual, and an external attribution in which responsibility for the outcome is related to some property of the situation or another person. The internal alternatives can be divided into those that attribute outcome to ability and those that attribute it to motivation. A number of studies have shown that students who persist on academic tasks take more personal responsibility for both successes and failures than do nonpersisters. In addition, persisters have been shown to believe that success is due to effort, while nonpersisters believe that success is due to ability and failure to lack of ability (Luchow, Crowe, & Kahn, 1985).

## Review of Research

A number of studies have found that students' attributions for their academic outcomes follow two general patterns: (1) a mastery pattern in which success is attributed to internal factors such as ability and failure is attributed to external factors or to lack of effort, and (2) a learned helplessness pattern in which students make stable attributions such as lack of ability to explain failure and externalize success (Diener & Dweck, 1978; Levesque & Lowe, 1992). Students who have experienced a great deal of failure (low achievers, learning disabled students, students with low self-concepts) tend to show a learned helplessness pattern (Levesque & Lowe, in press).

The early study by Dweck (1975) on the effectiveness of attribution retraining in changing maladaptive attributional patterns, described above, was replicated by a number of investigators in attempts to refine and extend the findings. Rhodes (1977) found that the performance of learned helpless children improved on training tasks as well as on generalization tasks after eighteen sessions of attribution retraining. Shustack and Fields (1980) found that attribution retraining paired with successful performance decreased deteriorations in performance when failure was presented, but they also found that continuous success experiences without attribution retraining did not decrease learned helpless behaviors. Chapin and Dyck (1976) compared the effects of continuous successes followed by reinforcement, interspersed successes and failures, and interspersed successes and failures with attribution retraining. Attribution retraining consisted of telling the children that they were trying hard when they succeeded and that they should have tried harder when they failed. Subjects were underachieving fifth, sixth, and seventh graders. Children who had received the partial reinforcement plus attribution retraining showed the greatest persistence.

Cecil and Medway (1986) reviewed the research literature on attribution retraining with low-achieving and learned helpless children. They concluded that attribution retraining that involves effort feedback is beneficial in increasing task persistence and academic performance of children with learning problems. In addition, they concluded that attribution retraining, either alone or in combination with partial reinforcement, is more effective than continuous reinforcement of success. They caution, however, that the studies have lacked follow-up measures; therefore, the durability of these effects has not been established.

In a review of the research on causal attributions of mentally retarded and learning disabled students, Borkowski, Weyhing, and Turner (1986) found that such children who attribute failure to a lack of ability are less likely to persist on a task. They also concluded that attribution retraining is an important component of programs that help educationally handicapped children learn strategy use and self-control.

A study conducted by Reid and Borkowski (1987) with hyperactive children confirms this conclusion. Seventy-seven hyperactive second, third, and fourth graders participated in this investigation, which compared the effectiveness of three training conditions. Children in a self-control condition received self-management training and instruction in the use of specific learning strategies. Children in a self-control plus attribution condition received self-management and strategy training plus training designed to enhance general and program-specific beliefs about the importance of effort in improving performance. Children in a control condition received strategy training, but no self-management or attribution training. The attribution training component focused on enhancing antecedent and program-generated self-attributions. Antecedent attributions represent pervasive self-perceptions about the causes of learning, while program-generated attributions represent attributions related to the immediate intervention program and task. Children who participated in attribution retraining used more complex learning strategies, displayed reduced impulsivity, and had higher effort endorsement scores on a measure of personal causality. Ten months following training, children in the self-control plus attribution condition persisted in their use of acquired learning strategies, maintained beliefs about the importance of effort, and displayed more mature memory knowledge. The authors concluded that the results supported the use of attribution and self-control training in treating deficits in learning strategies in hyperactive and learning disabled students.

A study by Thomas and Pashley (1982) extended the use of

attribution retraining procedures from specially trained experimenters/instructors (as had typically been the case) to special education classroom teachers. In this study, teachers were taught to conduct attribution retraining programs in their classrooms, and the programs resulted in improved persistence among the learning disabled children who received training.

Although attribution retraining has been suggested as a component of treatment for depressed youngsters, only one study has documented its effectiveness. Stark, Reynolds, and Kaslow (1987) assigned twenty-nine moderately to severely depressed nine- to twelve-year-olds to either a self-control, behavioral problem-solving, or waiting list control condition. The self-control condition was designed to teach the children skills for self-monitoring, self-evaluating performance, attributing the cause of good and bad outcomes, and self-consequating. The skills were taught through didactic presentations, exercises, and behavioral homework assignments. Children who participated in the self-control and behavioral problem-solving treatments showed significant improvements on self-report and interview measures of depression while children in the control condition did not. Results were maintained at eight-week follow-up assessment.

## Summary

Attribution retraining is a cognitive-behavioral approach to building coping skills that has been shown to be effective in helping low-achieving students cope with academic tasks and failure and in helping depressed youngsters cope with a variety of negative events. Use of attribution retraining with low-achieving students appears to be especially amenable to classroom implementation, as the procedure is relatively straightforward and easy to integrate into a classroom instructional routine. With depressed youngsters, however, attribution retraining should be implemented by helping professionals as one component of the multicomponent intervention program that is needed to deal with the complex problems of these children and adolescents.

Attribution retraining typically has two elements: (1) the trainee is intermittently exposed to failure, and (2) the trainee is taught to attribute the failure to insufficient effort. Effort attributions are taught by telling the trainee that failure was due to his or her not trying hard enough.

Those who have reviewed the research literature on attribution retraining indicate that the training needs to be intensive, prolonged, and consistent to counteract existing negative beliefs regarding causation that have built up over an extended period of time. It has also been recommended that initial attribution retraining focus on task-specific beliefs, and that training gradually begin to address more general attributional beliefs (Borkowski, Weyhing, & Turner, 1986). A number of authors have raised concern about conveying the idea that the only requirement for success is effort when in fact there are many tasks for which increased effort will not be sufficient for success (Licht, 1983). In response to this concern, recent investigators have been examining the effects of attributing failure of low-achieving students to ineffective use of strategies as well as lack of effort (Reid & Borkowski, 1987).

A substantial number of efficacy studies have been conducted regarding this method of building coping skills; these have been fairly consistent in reporting gains during and immediately after training. However, very few studies have examined the durability of these effects, indicating a significant need for continued examination of the potential for long-term effectiveness with this type of intervention.

*Ten*

# Promoting
# Behavioral Self-Control

The ability to direct and change one's own behavior provides a foundation for developing constructive responses to potential stressors and for incorporating other coping skills into an individual's behavioral repertoire. Behavioral self-management training (also called behavioral self-control training) teaches children and adolescents to use behavior modification techniques, based on operant conditioning principles, as a means of achieving goals or addressing their behavioral or emotional problems.

This approach to building coping skills consists of training individuals to assess and evaluate their own behavior, set goals, arrange their environment in a manner that will encourage goal attainment, and reward themselves when they achieve goals. The aims of this type of coping skills intervention have been extremely wide ranging and have included improving various types of academic skills (reading, mathematics, handwriting), increasing prosocial behaviors, and decreasing aggression, classroom disruptive behaviors, and depression.

## Development

Behavioral self-management training has its roots in the literature on learning theory and operant conditioning, which emphasize the importance of environmental contingencies and consequences in eliciting and maintaining behavior. Initial research on the use of operant techniques to treat problems of children and adolescents focused on procedures in which a therapist, classroom teacher, or parent observed and evaluated the behavior of the child or adolescent and administered consequences. However, as early as 1953, B. F. Skinner raised the issue of self-management by indicating that individuals might be able to control their behavior by dispensing their own reinforcers contingent upon certain behavioral responses. He stated that an individual could control himself or herself "precisely as he would control the behavior of anyone else—through the manipulation of variables of which behavior is a function" (p. 228).

Much of the initial research examining and establishing the effects of behavioral self-management procedures was conducted in the 1970s. In the early 1970s Frederick Kanfer and his colleagues described and studied a three-stage model that identified the major components of behavioral self-management (Kanfer, 1970; Kanfer & Karoly, 1982; Kanfer & Phillips, 1970). This model included self-observation, self-evaluation, and self-consequation. Self-observation occurs when individuals observe and record their own behavior. Self-evaluation occurs when individuals monitor their target behavior and compare it to a criterion level. Self-consequation consists of the contingent delivery of rewarding or punishing consequences to oneself.

In 1972, David Watson and Roland Tharp published the first of many editions of *Self-Directed Behavior: Self Modification for Personal Adjustment,* a book designed to acquaint the public, as well as professionals, with behavioral self-management procedures. A major premise of this book was that in order to change, individuals need to develop the ability to change the antecedents and consequences that affect their behavior, by first noticing them and then devising a plan to change them. In a recent edition of this book (Watson & Tharp, 1985) the authors indicate that there is a sequence that all successful self-management programs follow:

1.  Select a goal and specify the behaviors that need to be changed in order to meet the goal.
2.  Make observations of those target behaviors.
3.  Devise a plan for change, applying psychological knowledge.
4.  Readjust your plan as you evaluate your progress.

Gross and Drabman (1982) delineate a number of reasons for the growing popularity of behavioral self-management training with school populations, as compared to the use of behavior modification procedures, in which teachers and/or parents administer the procedures and control the contingencies. They state that when parents, teachers, or other individuals control the contingencies, they may miss a large number of instances of the occurrence of the target behavior, leading to a low probability that the response will be consistently reinforced, a condition necessary for behavior change. They also point out that individuals who administer the contingencies may become discriminative stimuli. If this situation occurs, the child may perform the target behavior only in the presence of the adult who delivers reinforcers. They also contend that procedures through which children are taught to control their own behavior will lead to stronger maintenance effects than if behavioral change is obtained through external control. Finally, they suggest that if children can be taught to control their own behavior, teachers can spend more time focusing on academic skills.

### Procedures

As stated above, behavioral self-management training involves teaching individuals to conduct three major procedures: self-observation, self-evaluation, and self-consequation. Approaches to behavioral self-management training with children and adolescents have ranged from allowing the child to control one or more of the three major components (observation, evaluation, reinforcement) of a behavior management program to training him or her in the entire range of procedures that make up behavioral self-management programs (Brigham, 1989). The procedures can be used in attempts to change behavior initiated by significant adult others, or after

training, by the individual child or adolescent, as a means of coping
with various problems and stress-producing situations.

## Self-Observation

Self-observation, also called self-monitoring or self-recording, is a
procedure through which students monitor and record instances of
their own specific behaviors. Thus, it is a two-step process in which
individuals determine the presence or absence of their own target
behavior, and the instances of the behavior are self-recorded (Nelson, 1977). Self-observation can be both an assessment technique
and a behavior change technique. The act of observing and recording one's behavior is frequently associated with a change in that
behavior. This is called reactivity. For example, if children are asked
to notice and record the number of times they call out in class without raising their hands, those acts of self-observation may decrease
calling-out behavior. Behavioral diaries, frequency self-recording,
and interval self-recording are three types of self-observation procedures typically used as part of behavioral self-management programs.

Use of a behavioral diary involves having the student describe, on a note pad, the circumstances surrounding the emission
of a target behavior each time that behavior occurs. The student is
usually taught to write a description of the antecedent events surrounding the behavior, the behavior itself, and the consequences
that occurred as a result of the behavior. For example, if a student
gets into fights at school he would be asked to write a description
of each fighting incident including (1) the physical setting, (2) the
individuals present before the fight started, (3) the behavior of the
individuals present before the fight, (4) the student's own behavior
immediately before and during the fight, and (5) events that occurred and the manner in which individuals behaved toward the
student after the fight. Multiple descriptions of antecedents, behaviors, and consequences provide information that can be used to
determine changes in settings and consequences that should be
made in order to effect behavioral change.

Frequency self-recording requires the child or adolescent to
keep a record of the number of times the target behavior occurs. For
example, a child might keep a record reflecting the number of times

she gets out of her seat without permission, is late for class, completes a math problem, or finishes her homework. The frequency count is typically done on a recording sheet or with a mechanical counter. If classroom behavior is being noted, the recording sheets can be taped to the student's desk for easy access.

Interval self-recording or time sampling occurs when individuals record whether they engaged in a specific behavior during a specified period of time. It is used for behaviors that are continuous (occur over long periods of time) rather than discrete (occur in individual units), or with behaviors that occur so often that frequency recording would be aversive. When interval self-recording is used, a block of time is divided into smaller time intervals and the individual is asked to record whether the behavior occurred during each interval. Alternatively, the individual might be asked to record whether he or she is engaging in the target behavior at the end of the interval. Interval self-recording is frequently used to monitor on-task behavior in the classroom. For example, a teacher might set a timer for ten minutes, and when the bell rings, ask students to record whether they were on task.

Duration self-recording is used when the length of occurrence of the behavior is of importance. Duration recording simply consists of noting how long the behavior lasted, using some type of watch or clock. For example, a student may be asked to record the length of time he or she studies or works on homework each night.

In order for self-observational procedures to be implemented appropriately and accurately, children and adolescents need to be trained in their use. This training should involve a number of steps such as these:

1.  Discussion of the use and importance of self-observation
2.  Selection and definition of the target behavior, including a discussion of characteristics of the target behavior, and role-play of accurate and inaccurate instances of the target behavior
3.  Selection of an appropriate and easily usable self-recording procedure
4.  Modeling of the use of the self-recording procedure
5.  Rehearsal of the use of the self-recording procedure
6.  Reinforcement of appropriate instances of self-recording dur-

ing training, with students rewarded when their records match those of an objective observer

The accuracy of self-recording after training can be maintained by having occasional checks for accuracy in which the student's record is compared to that of an objective observer. In addition, reinforcement for accurate self-recording after training can maintain accuracy.

### Self-Evaluation

As stated above, self-evaluation occurs after self-monitoring when an individual evaluates his or her behavior against a criterion. To illustrate, Jonathan may have set a criterion level of reading three chapters in an assigned book each night. He would compare the actual number of chapters read per night to this level. Cautela (1971) contends that behavior changes may occur as a result of such self-evaluation alone because when an individual compares his or her behavior to a criterion level, self-reinforcing or self-punishing statements will be made as a result of that comparison. However, research investigating the effectiveness of this procedure indicates that self-evaluation alone is not an effective means of changing behavior, although it can be effective when combined with other components of behavioral self-management (Gross & Drabman, 1982).

Workman (1982) describes the use of self-ratings to assist students to evaluate their behavior. This intervention involves teaching students to rate their behavior according to a rating scale. After a target behavior and criterion level are defined, students are asked to rate their behavior during a specific time interval on a three- or five-point scale in relation to whether the criterion level for the behavior was met. The level of performance required for each point on the scale is defined and explained to the students. As an illustration, students may be asked to rate themselves every five minutes on a five-point scale according to how well they have been paying attention to a presentation, with 0 equaling not well at all, 1 equaling fairly well, and 2 equaling very well.

Graphing the results of self-recording may also help children and adolescents evaluate their behavior. Graphs can provide visual evidence that behavior change is occurring and that behavior is consistent with or approaching criterion levels. Simple line graphs are typically used to plot the frequency or duration of a behavior across time. Figure 10.1 shows an example of a graph that illustrates behavioral improvement relative to a specific criterion.

As with self-recording, the accuracy of self-evaluation can be increased through training sessions in which students are rewarded when their self-evaluations match the evaluations of an objective observer. After an initial training period in which rewards are obtained for matching evaluations, this procedure can also be monitored periodically during the implementation of a behavioral self-management program to ensure a continuing high level of accuracy.

## Self-Reward

Although the original theoretical literature on self-management described self-consequation as the administering of both rewards and punishment to oneself, the literature on child and adolescent self-management has focused on self-reward, contingent upon a

**Figure 10.1. Graphing Behavioral Improvement.**

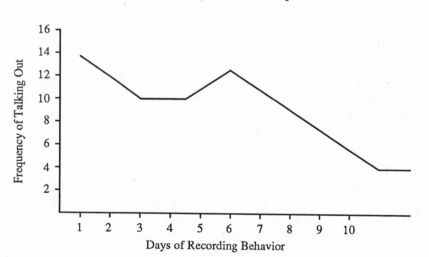

specific behavior, as the only aspect of self-consequation appropriate for use with this population. Glynn, Thomas, and Shee (1973) defined two aspects of self-reward in behavioral self-management programs. The first is self-determination of reinforcement in which the individual determines the nature and amount of reinforcer he or she should receive contingent upon performance of specific behavior. The second is self-administration of reinforcement in which the individual dispenses his or her own reinforcers, which may or may not be self-determined, contingent upon performance of specific behavior. There are two main types of self-reward: overt self-reward and covert self-reward.

Overt self-rewards can take a variety of forms, as rewards do in externally administered behavior modification programs. In self-management programs conducted by children and adolescents, token reinforcers, activity reinforcers, and object reinforcers are typically used. Token reinforcers usually consist of chips, check marks, or points that are self-administered contingent on desirable behavior; these can be accumulated and traded for concrete objects or participation in desired activities.

As with other programs based on operant principles, a reinforcer should be selected because of its value and motivating properties for the target student. In addition, ease of administration is also important in considering whether a particular reinforcer should be used.

Gross and Drabman (1982) indicate that token programs are the most commonly used type of reward system in child and adolescent self-management programs. There are numerous reasons for this. Youths can easily give themselves tokens without disrupting others in the class. Numerous back-up reinforcers, for which the tokens are traded, can be used in such programs. This system reduces the probability that the young person will become bored or sated with the program. In addition, as behavior and criterion levels change, the exchange rates between tokens and back-up reinforcers can be adjusted so that consumption of large amounts of reinforcers does not become a problem. Finally, gradually increasing the exchange rates and fading the use of tokens can increase the probability that behavioral change will be maintained over time.

Workman (1982) contends that covert self-rewards can also be

used in behavioral self-management programs. Covert positive reinforcement consists of having the student imagine being in a
situation in which a specific appropriate behavior is needed, engaging in the appropriate behavior, and, as a result, experiencing a
highly pleasurable sensation. Workman (1982, pp. 85–86) provides
the following example of teaching students this procedure:

> Step 1. Tell your students to imagine themselves
> in the situation where you want their behavior to im-
> prove. For example, you might say, "I want everyone to
> close your eyes and imagine yourself in this class. Now
> imagine that I am telling you to take out your reading
> workbooks to do the assignment."
>
> Step 2. Then, have your students imagine them-
> selves successfully engaging in a behavior that is appro-
> priate to the above classroom situation. For example,
> "Now imagine yourselves taking out your workbook and
> really working hard on the reading assignment. Be sure
> that you keep your eyes closed and imagine this as clearly
> as possible."
>
> Step 3. During the final step, instruct your stu-
> dents to imagine one of the highly positive events from
> their lists. For example, "Now, imagine yourself getting
> to meet all the stars of your favorite television show.
> Imagine that you're really excited, and the stars are all
> talking with you and being friendly."

## Review of Research

A sizable body of research literature examines the effectiveness of
behavioral self-management programs in helping children and adolescents cope with problems and effect emotional and behavioral
change. Some of these studies investigate the effectiveness of the
various components or combinations of components of behavioral
self-management programs in improving academic or social behaviors. Others examine the efficacy of training in the entire behavioral
self-management process as an approach to building coping skills,
and to preventing and treating emotional and behavioral problems.

## Self-Observation

A number of studies indicate that self-monitoring and self-recording alone can result in changes in behavior. In a very early study, use of self-recording increased attending in an eighth-grade girl and decreased talking out in class in an eighth-grade boy (Broden, Hall, & Mitts, 1971). The girl was given a recording sheet in history class and told to mark whether she was studying "whenever she thought of it." She was praised by the school counselor, and later in the study by the teacher, for appropriate behavior; improvements in her behavior were maintained over a three-week follow-up. Although the boy's behavior improved initially with use of self-observation, the improvement was not maintained.

Gottman and McFall (1972) increased classroom participation of students at risk for dropping out of high school by having them record instances of speaking during class discussions. Piersel and Kratochwill (1979) improved the number of class assignments completed by a fifteen-year-old hyperactive boy by having him self-record, on notebook paper, the number of reading units he completed each day. In a study with a much younger subject, Hallahan, Lloyd, Kosiewicz, Kauffman, and Graves (1979) found that self-monitoring and recording increased the on-task behavior of a seven-year-old with attentional problems. The student had been instructed to self-record whether he was paying attention each time a tape-recorded tone sounded.

Mace and Shea (1990) have reviewed the research regarding the effectiveness of self-monitoring and self-recording and have concluded that eight variables are potential contributors to the effects of these procedures on behavior (reactivity).

1. The procedure is more likely to be effective with students who are motivated to change their behavior.
2. Positive behaviors are likely to increase and negative behaviors are likely to decrease as a result of self-monitoring and self-recording.
3. Effects are likely to be more pronounced for conspicuous non-verbal behaviors and for undesirable behaviors with reliable

antecedents (behaviors that occur consistently after a specific event).

4.  Behavior change is more likely to occur if, along with self-monitoring and self-recording, performance goals are set, feedback is given on these goals, and self-recording is reinforced.

5.  Some studies indicate that behavior change is more likely if self-recording is done before the target behavior occurs (urges to call out in class are recorded rather than actual verbalizations).

6.  Behavior change becomes less likely as the number of behaviors that are self-recorded increases.

7.  Behavior change is more likely if the student self-records continuously (in all classes) rather than intermittently (in only some classes).

8.  Use of obtrusive (easily noticeable) recording devices, such as a piece of paper taped to the top of a student's desk, increases the likelihood that behavior will change.

## Self-Evaluation

A number of studies have shown that self-evaluation is an important component of a behavioral self-management program; however, this procedure does not appear to be effective when used by itself. A study conducted by Santogrossi, O'Leary, Romanczyk, and Kaufman (1973) illustrates this point. Disruptive adolescents were taught to self-evaluate their classroom behavior and award themselves points. No back-up reinforcers were associated with these points, and the self-evaluation procedure had no effect on the disruptive behavior. Teacher-determined points with back-up reinforcers were subsequently used and resulted in a substantial decline in disruptiveness. In a study conducted with third graders, the effectiveness of self-evaluation in improving writing skills was examined (Ballard & Glynn, 1975). Self-evaluation alone had no effect on accuracy of writing, but when reinforcement was made contingent on accuracy of writing, large improvements occurred in that behavior.

Spates and Kanfer (1977) conducted a study demonstrating that self-evaluation can be an important component of a behavioral self-management program. First-grade students were assigned to experimental groups that were trained in different combinations of the components of the self-management process (self-monitoring, self-evaluation, and self-reinforcement) in an attempt to increase accurate completion of arithmetic tasks. Children in groups that used self-evaluation only, or self-evaluation combined with other components, performed better than those in groups that did not use self-evaluation.

A study of behaviorally handicapped elementary school children conducted by Rhode, Morgan, and Young (1983) showed that self-evaluation, combined with other behavioral procedures, could be effective in promoting generalization and maintenance of behavior change. A token reinforcement program was used to increase student rule-following behavior. A self-evaluation program in which students rated their behavior on a six-point scale at fifteen-minute intervals was used to generalize gains made in the students' resource room to their regular classroom. If self-ratings were within one point of teacher ratings, students could award themselves points to be exchanged for toys and snacks. After the matching procedure was gradually faded, behavioral gains were found to generalize to and maintain in the regular classroom.

*Self-Reward*

Numerous school-based studies with children and adolescents have documented the effectiveness of self-reward in producing behavioral change. These studies have been done with children and adolescents in regular classroom settings as well as with those in special classroom settings; they have addressed academic as well as social behaviors.

A few studies have found positive effects of self-determined reinforcement. In a very early study, Lovitt and Curtiss (1969) found that self-determined reinforcement was more effective than teacher-determined reinforcement in improving academic task completion in a twelve-year-old behaviorally disordered student. Frederiksen and Frederiksen (1975) compared the effects of both teacher-determined and self-determined reinforcement with sixth and seventh graders whose IQs were between 50 and 80. Target behaviors included task completion and disruptive behavior. Self-determined reinforcement was shown to be equal to teacher-determined reinforcement in increasing task completion, and to be better than teacher-determined reinforcement in decreasing disruptive behavior.

On-task behavior has also been shown to improve through use of self-administered reinforcement. Glynn, Thomas, and Shee (1973) found that, with second graders, a combination of self-recording and self-administered reinforcement led to improvements in on-task behaviors, such as looking at the teacher, reading to the teacher, and taking part in class discussions. Students rewarded themselves with points that could be exchanged for free-time activities. These investigators also found that although an external reinforcement program led to improved on-task behavior as well, the behavioral self-management procedures resulted in greater improvements. Glynn and Thomas (1974) found similarly positive results when a combination of self-recording and self-administered reinforcement was used with third graders who had severe attention problems.

A number of studies have addressed improving academic skills. Among these, a 1975 study by Ballard and Glynn illustrated that self-administered reinforcement could improve story writing of elementary school children. The children self-recorded the number of sentences, action words, and describing words they used in a daily story-writing exercise. Later in the study, they delivered token points to themselves as rewards. The investigators found that self-recording alone had little effect on the children's behavior; however, substantial increases in the target behaviors resulted after the self-reward system was introduced. Self-administered reinforcement has also been shown to increase reading accuracy of second graders (Humphrey, Karoly, & Kirshchenbaum, 1978), improve math performance of ninth graders (Glynn, 1970), and improve performance of fourth graders on tests in history, Spanish language, and reading comprehension (Wall, 1982).

Improvement in academic performance has been shown with special education students as well as with those in regular classrooms. Kapadia and Fantuzzo (1988) illustrated the use of self-administered reinforcement with learning disabled students by exposing them to two different types of reinforcement conditions: one in which the teacher awarded points for correct spelling, and the other in which the students awarded themselves points for correct spelling. The points could be exchanged for back-up reinforcers. The investigators found that both teacher- and self-awarded points improved students' spelling accuracy, although the self-reinforcement condition yielded greater improvements.

Self-administered reinforcement has also been used to decrease disruptive social behaviors in the classroom. For example, Bolstad and Johnson (1972) used a combination of self-recording and self-reinforcement to reduce high rates of talking-out, hitting others, and out-of-seat behavior in first and second graders.

In reviewing research on self-reward, Gross and Drabman (1982) found that a number of variables contribute to its effectiveness. Prior exposure to externally controlled reinforcement or to other children involved in self-reward programs may enhance the effectiveness of self-reward and make the procedure easier to teach. In addition, exposure to externally controlled reinforcement provides an opportunity to build matching experiences into the training procedure for self-administration of rewards. Matching procedures have been found to prevent lenient and noncontingent self-delivery of rewards. The effectiveness of self-reward may also be increased by establishing achievement standards of increasing difficulty through which target behaviors are broken into components and shaped.

### Multicomponent Programs

Although the objective of self-management training is to make children and adolescents managers of their own behavior, only a small number of studies have examined the use of behavioral self-management training as an approach to building coping skills in children and adolescents that can be used to deal with problems and situations beyond those initially targeted for intervention. Thomas Brigham and his colleagues have completed a few studies in this area and Brigham has recently published a treatment manual for professionals, along with an accompanying student manual that describes the behavioral self-management approach to building coping skills (Brigham, 1989).

In an initial study of behavioral self-management training,

Gross, Brigham, Hopper, and Bologna (1980) taught predelinquent youths a course in behavioral self-management. The course contained ten lessons on the principles and procedures of behavior analysis. Students were required to implement a self-change project as well as a behavior modification project in which they altered another person's behavior. The participants learned the principles and procedures presented in the course, successfully altered their own behavior as well as that of another person, and showed reductions in delinquent behavior. Other studies of this type of training program have found that it has resulted in decreases in disruptive classroom behavior in high school students (Brigham, 1989), success in job acquisition for high school dropouts enrolled in a high school equivalency diploma program (Brigham, Contreras, Handel, & Castillo, 1983), and decreases in detentions of sixth, seventh, and eighth graders (Brigham, Hopper, Hill, de Armas, & Newsom, 1985).

The behavioral self-management training approach has also been used to treat depression in children and adolescents. These individuals tend to self-monitor negative events to the exclusion of positive events; set excessively high, unattainable standards for performance; fail to self-reinforce sufficiently; and self-punish more than normal youngsters. Self-management training for depressed youngsters focuses on teaching them to self-monitor pleasant events; set realistic, acceptable standards of performance and evaluate discrepancies between their standards for performance and their evaluation of their performance; and self-reward contingent on their displaying nondepressive behavior (Reynolds & Stark, 1986). Reynolds and Coats (1986) reported successful use of behavioral self-management training that included instruction in self-monitoring, self-evaluation, and self-reinforcement with moderately and severely depressed adolescents. The training—10 one-hour sessions conducted over a five-week period in a high school—resulted in decreases in depressive symptomatology that were maintained at a five-week follow-up assessment. Stark, Reynolds, and Kaslow (1987) reported that moderately depressed nine- to twelve-year-olds improved on self-report and interview measures of depression as a result of self-management training consisting of twelve 45-

to 50-minute sessions conducted over five weeks. The improvements maintained at eight-week follow-up assessment.

## Summary

Behavioral self-management training has been shown to be an effective approach to assisting children and adolescents in coping with a variety of potentially stressful situations and reducing behavioral and emotional problems. This type of training teaches skills in self-observation, self-evaluation, and self-consequation. Self-observation has been found to be effective alone or in combination with the other self-management components in changing behavior.

Most research completed to date has documented the effectiveness of individual components or combinations of components of behavioral self-management training in dealing with intervention targets identified by significant adults in the youngster's school or home environment. However, the greatest potential for this type of training appears to be in the possibilities it offers youngsters to build personal coping skills that can be used to address a variety of problems that are self-identified. Although the theoretical and practice-oriented literature regarding this type of use is expanding, a more extensive evaluation of this approach to building coping skills is needed for its effectiveness to be definitively established.

*Eleven*

# Prevention Applications

As indicated in previous chapters, coping skills interventions can be useful in treating a variety of child and adolescent emotional and behavioral problems. In addition, these types of interventions have been found especially useful in preventing such problems. Preventive interventions have been advocated by a variety of scientists, practitioners, professional associations, and federal agencies as desirable and effective ways to reduce the frequency and severity of mental health problems in the child and adolescent population (Zins & Forman, 1988).

Because of their access to virtually the entire child population at an early age, schools have the potential to effect major positive changes in children and adolescents by providing preventive interventions as part of the curriculum. Coping skills interventions are especially amenable for use in school-based prevention programs as they teach students skills they can use to direct and control their lives. Three major problem areas that have been targets of intervention programs using preventive coping skills will be described in this chapter: adolescent alcohol and other drug abuse,

145

effects of adolescent sexual behavior including pregnancy and sexually transmitted diseases, and adolescent suicide. In addition, the potential use of coping skills programs to prevent disorders resulting from the experience of catastrophic situations will be explored. Finally, the use of coping skills programs to promote general emotional and social competence and thereby prevent emotional and social problems will be described.

## Alcohol and Other Drug Use

Numerous surveys have documented alcohol and other drug use as a major problem for this nation's adolescents. The National Institute on Drug Abuse (1991), using 1990 data, reported that 40.7 percent of high school seniors have used marijuana, 64.4 percent have used cigarettes, and 89.5 percent have used alcohol. Although the percentage of youth involved in drug use has declined during the past decade, the use rates remain problematic and higher than those in other industrialized nations (Forman & Linney, 1988).

In a review of coping skills interventions aimed at preventing alcohol and other drug use in adolescents, Forman and Linney (1991) describe two types of programs. One focuses on teaching adolescents skills that can be used to deal with social influence and pressure. The other focuses on teaching interpersonal and intrapersonal coping skills that can be used to deal with the wide variety of social, psychological, and behavioral factors that influence drug abuse.

The social influence programs are largely based on the identification of peer pressure as a significant cause of drug abuse. The foundation for these programs is the principle of social inoculation, which assumes that resistance to social pressure to use drugs will be greater if the adolescent has had experience in dealing with this pressure in a controlled setting (Evans, 1976). These programs have also commonly been called "Saying No" programs and typically include instruction in recognizing peer pressure and learning strategies for resisting peer pressure based on assertiveness training techniques. The programs usually contain numerous role-play exercises of common situations in which there is social pressure for adolescents to use drugs. Practice in these role-play situations is designed to "inoculate" the student against similar situations outside the training session.

Horan and Williams (1982) used assertiveness training as a way to prevent alcohol and other drug use. In their study, nonassertive junior high school students participated in groups, conducted by counselors, that met for five 45-minute sessions over two weeks. One-third of the training exercises focused on situations involving peer pressure to use drugs. Students who participated in this program showed gains on behavioral and psychometric measures of assertiveness as well as decreased willingness to use alcohol and marijuana. At three-year follow-up, the students continued to display higher levels of assertiveness and less self-reported drug use than students in no-treatment or placebo control conditions.

The Waterloo Smoking Prevention Program (Flay, d'Avernas, Best, Kersell, & Ryan, 1983) was a social influence program for sixth graders. It was structured in six weekly sessions of one hour each held at the beginning of the school year, two booster sessions at the end of the school year, two booster sessions at the beginning of grade 7, and one booster session at the beginning of grade 8. The program was delivered to students by health educators and had three components. The first focused on the reasons not to smoke and the consequences of smoking. The second focused on the social influences that encourage smoking and on skills to resist those influences. Social coping skills were taught, role-played, and practiced. The third component focused on decision making and public commitment. An evaluation of this program, conducted with 697 children in twenty-two schools, indicated reduced onset of smoking as well as increases in the number of children who stopped smoking.

Pentz (1985) illustrated the effectiveness of drug use prevention programs based on training assertiveness skills. This program consisted of seven 55-minute sessions and taught students assertiveness skills that they could use in everyday situations with teachers, parents, and peers. After participation in this training, sixth- through ninth-grade students increased on measures of social competence and self-efficacy as well as in grade point average; they decreased in onset rates for alcohol use.

Training programs in broad-spectrum coping skills have also provided evidence of effectiveness in the research literature on preventing alcohol and other drug use in adolescents. Schinke and Gilchrist (1984) describe a program called Cognitive-Behavioral Skills Training that provides students with general personal and social coping skills as well as techniques specific to situations in which they may be pressured to use cigarettes. The eight-session program, delivered in one-hour blocks, includes instruction in smoking-related health information, decision making and problem solving, self-instruction techniques, and assertive communication. When used with sixth graders, this program has resulted in improvements on measures of problem solving, decision-making skills, assertiveness skills, smoking knowledge and attitudes, and intentions to smoke in the future.

Botvin (1983, 1989) also describes a coping skills training program, called Life Skills Training, which teaches general coping skills as well as skills and knowledge specifically related to alcohol and other drug use. The program is typically conducted in twelve weekly sessions and consists of five components. The first is a cognitive component with information regarding prevalence, causes, and consequences of tobacco, alcohol, and marijuana use. The second addresses decision making. An anxiety management component focuses on cognitive and behavioral techniques such as imagery and physical relaxation. A social skills training component includes general social and communication skills as well as assertiveness techniques that can be used to resist peer pressure. Finally, a self-improvement component provides students with the principles of self-management. A number of studies have indicated that this program can have significant effects on drug use in adolescents (Botvin, 1987; Botvin, Baker, Renick, Filazzola, and Botvin, 1984; Botvin & Eng, 1982; Botvin, Eng, & Williams, 1980; Botvin, Renick, & Baker, 1983).

Forman and Linney (1991) describe a multicomponent drug abuse prevention program for high-risk youth based on Botvin's Life Skills Training. The program includes student training, teacher training, and parent training components; it has the goal of teaching the participants constructive methods of dealing with problems and stress so that they can resist peer pressure to use drugs and will not turn to drug use as an inappropriate avoidant coping response.

During the ten sessions of this program, students receive information about drug use and learn coping skills in four areas: (1) behavioral self-management, (2) emotional self-management (relaxation skills, rational-emotive skills, self-instruction skills), (3) decision making, and (4) interpersonal communication (assertiveness skills, peer resistance, communication skills, social skills.) The teacher training component of this program works to enhance generalization of behavior change in students by training school staff to encourage use of coping skills in the school setting. The parent training component teaches parents to encourage use of coping skills in the home setting. Both the teacher and parent training components describe each coping skill taught to the students and provide information on how each skill can be encouraged through three methods: modeling, cuing, and reinforcing.

In a meta-analysis of the outcome results of 143 adolescent drug prevention programs, Tobler (1986) identified five different types of programs: knowledge only, affective only, peer programs, knowledge plus affective, and alternatives. Peer programs included those that taught assertive refusal skills as well as those that taught social and personal coping skills. These programs were found to be superior for the magnitude of their effects on all outcome measures for the average school-based population.

## Adolescent Sexual Behavior

Numerous recent news reports have underscored the problems associated with the consequences of adolescent sexual behavior. The prevalence of pregnancy and sexually transmitted diseases among adolescents has grown significantly and has resulted in increasingly serious effects. Over one million teenagers become pregnant each year, with recent marked increases among adolescents who are younger than fifteen years old (Westoff, Calcot, & Foster, 1983). Pregnancy is the greatest contributor to the school dropout rate for females (Strobino, 1987). In addition, infants born to adolescent mothers are at risk for a variety of medical, psychological, and social problems (Paget, 1988). Over the past decade, the occurrence of sexually transmitted diseases has also increased substantially, with

adolescents being one of the groups most at risk for syphilis, gonor-
rhea, and herpes (Babouri, 1985).

   Programs with coping skills training components have been
developed with the goal of enhancing sexual responsibility of adolescents and thereby reducing the prevalence of pregnancy and
sexually transmitted diseases. Implementation of these types of programs has been limited in school settings because of serious disagreements among the adult population regarding the appropriate
content of and setting for sex education programs. Despite these
obstacles resulting from political and moral disagreements, a small
number of programs have been implemented and evaluated. A
number of authors have stated that the prevalence of pregnancy and
sexually transmitted diseases is due as much to impulsive sexual
behaviors as to lack of information, and that if adolescents develop
a set of values and decision-making skills, they will approach sexuality in a reflective and more responsible manner (Paget, 1988).

   Howard (1983) describes a program called "Postponing Sexual Involvement" that is aimed at the general adolescent population
and emphasizes developing the ability to resist social pressure, including pressure from mass media messages and from peers in
groups and in individual situations. This program consists of four
90-minute sessions and teaches students problem solving and assertiveness skills as methods of dealing with social pressure. A number
of multicomponent community-based programs, such as Girls Club
of Dallas, also include training in assertiveness skills as one means
of assisting teens to deal constructively with their sexuality (Children's Defense Fund, 1987).

   Steven Schinke and Lewayne Gilchrist have written a
number of journal articles describing the procedures and evaluation
results of an interpersonal skills training approach to preventing
adolescent pregnancy (Schinke, 1982; Schinke, Blythe, & Gilchrist,
1981; Schinke & Gilchrist, 1977; Schinke, Gilchrist, & Blythe, 1980;
Schinke, Gilchrist, & Small, 1979). Their training program is based
on the premise that many adolescents become pregnant because they
lack cognitive and behavioral skills necessary to use information
related to sexual behavior and contraception. The program first
addresses basic information on human sexuality, reproduction, and
contraception. Participants then describe potential or actual prob-

lems related to dating and sexual activity. Next, participants are trained in problem-solving skills including generating alternatives, evaluating outcomes, and choosing a plan of action. Finally, students learn verbal and nonverbal assertiveness skills such as eye contact, body posture, gestures, voice volume, fluency, affect, positive self-statements, refusing unreasonable demands, requesting changes in another's behavior, and initiating interactions with peers, parents, and other adults. These skills are taught through coaching, role-play, feedback, and reinforcement using situations identified by the participants. Evaluations of this program indicate that participants increased on information, problem-solving, and assertiveness measures, and that they reported practicing more effective contraception than did students in control groups.

Babouri (1985) presents one of the only evaluations in the literature on programs aimed at preventing sexually transmitted diseases among adolescents. Participants in the group described in this study were adolescent girls, ages thirteen to seventeen. The girls participated in the group, conducted by a health educator at a health clinic, once a week, for one and one-half hours, for ten months. The group focused on building a peer support system, developing decision-making skills, clarifying values, and increasing their knowledge of human sexuality, sex information, and physiology. Results of the evaluation indicated that before the intervention, the girls in the experimental and control groups did not differ significantly in incidence of sexual activity or use of contraceptives; however, girls who participated in the training demonstrated no incident of contracting a sexually transmitted disease during or after group participation, while girls in the control condition showed an increasing incidence of contracting sexually transmitted diseases.

The growing incidence of acquired immune deficiency syndrome (AIDS) in the adolescent population gives increasing urgency to the development and implementation of programs aimed at preventing sexually transmitted diseases among these young people. Recent reports indicate that although the current number of reported cases of AIDS in adolescents is low, it is doubling each year. Many of the younger male cases were infected by blood transfusions, but young female cases are reported to be infected mostly through sexual contact. Young adults represent 20 percent of all

AIDS cases, and given the long incubation period for the virus, it is likely that many of these infections were transmitted during the teenage years (Brooks-Gunn, Boyer, & Hein, 1988).

Brooks-Gunn and others (1988) contend that given the seriousness of this problem and the likelihood of increasing prevalence rates, prevention programs that include education in the schools are essential. A recent survey has indicated that 94 percent of parents want to have education in the schools about human immunodeficiency virus (HIV) transmission (Meade, 1988). Brooks-Gunn and others (1988) suggest that this type of education should begin in elementary school and extend through secondary school; its content should focus on AIDS-related and human sexuality information as well as coping skills training in decision making, peer resistance, behavior skills, and self-inoculation. Longshore (1990) concurs that skills for risk reduction should be an essential component of AIDS education programs. These include interpersonal skills that help the adolescent resist the pressure to have sex or to use illegal drugs.

## Suicide

Suicide is the second leading cause of death among adolescents in the United States and the completed suicide rate among youth has been increasing steadily and substantially during the last forty years. Suicide attempts are significantly more common than completed suicides. Studies investigating suicide attempt rates have found between 8 percent and 20 percent of adolescents attempt suicide. Rates of suicidal ideation are even higher, with some surveys indicating incidence to be in the 50 percent to 65 percent range (Davis & Sandoval, 1991).

Stress has been identified as one of the major contributors to suicidality in children and adolescents (Cohen-Sandler, Berman, & King, 1982). Rubenstein (1989) reports that during the year prior to a teenager's suicide attempt, his or her stress scores have been 33 percent higher than those of nonsuicidal adolescents. The types of stress that increase the probability of suicide include stress related to sexuality, achievement pressure, family suicide, and personal loss.

Researchers have also found that suicidal children and adolescents are not as adept at interpersonal problem solving as nonsuicidal individuals (Platt, Spivack, & Bloom, 1971). In addition, suicidal youth are less likely to generate active cognitive coping strategies (Asarnow, Carlson, & Guthrie, 1987), use social withdrawal more often as a coping mechanism (Spirito, Stark, & Williams, 1988), are less able to cope with angry and sad feelings, and are less able to think through the consequences of their actions (Kahn, 1989). Beck (1976) has attempted to explain suicidal behavior through a cognitive triad model suggesting that many suicidal individuals have a negative view of themselves, a negative view of the world, and a negative view of the future or a sense of hopelessness.

Development of coping skills has been used as one approach to preventing suicide. Suicide prevention programs that focus on such skills have included components on stress reduction, social skills development, general problem solving, and critical thinking (Davis, Sandoval, & Wilson, 1988). In addition, because of the cognitive factors that appear to be related to suicide, many treatment efforts focus on changing the manner in which the individuals view themselves and situations in which they are involved.

### Effects of Disaster and Trauma

In the past few years, increasing attention has been given to the mental health disturbances of children and adolescents that may develop as a result of catastrophic events including natural and human-induced disaster, hostage taking, molestation, physical abuse, and physical assault. Gist and Lubin (1989) found a range of psychological and behavioral symptoms that may occur in children as a result of exposure to disastrous events; these include sleep disorders, persistent thoughts of the trauma, belief that another traumatic event will occur, conduct disturbances, hyperalertness, avoidance of anything symbolic of the event, psychophysiological disturbances, enuresis, thumbsucking, and dependent behavior. The authors also contend that children may be prone to develop these types of symptoms if their parents are affected by a disastrous event. Reports indicating the widespread prevalence of child abuse and the increase in numbers of children who are victims or observers of violent crime have underscored the need for methods of helping children and adolescents cope with such events. Children also need help in dealing with natural disasters such as the Buffalo Creek Dam disaster, the Xenia, Ohio, tornado, the nuclear accident at Three Mile Island, the eruption of Mount St. Helens, Hurricane Hugo, and a number of California earthquakes.

Some research literature indicates that maladaptive coping responses may exacerbate the effects of exposure to disastrous events or become problems in themselves, such as drug abuse (Silver & Wortman, 1980). Pynoos and Nader (1990) found that children vary in the ways they interpret the disastrous event, interpret their symptoms, regulate their emotions, and search for meaning, information, and assistance. Studies regarding the preventive and ameliorative effects of various types of coping skills training on populations exposed to or at risk of experiencing disaster have not yet been conducted. However, it appears likely that effective coping skills of children and the significant adults in their lives may moderate the effects of exposure to a disastrous event. Such preventive interventions can be implemented before, during, or after a disaster, and investigators who have studied posttraumatic reactions of children and adolescents have called for research in this area (Pynoos & Nader, 1990).

## Promotion of Emotional and Social Competence

The presence of coping skills, social supports, and positive self-esteem has been found to offset the risk of emotional and social problems posed by high stress and/or physical vulnerability in children and adolescents. The absence of these coping mechanisms increases the likelihood that emotional or behavioral disorders will occur even under conditions of moderate stress and no physical vulnerability (Albee, 1982). A number of investigators and authors, therefore, have underscored the importance of school-based programs that are preventive in nature and that aim to develop general emotional and social competence in children and adolescents (Elias & Branden, 1988).

Programs that focus on development of social-cognitive

problem solving are among the most frequently used and best developed for enhancement of general social and emotional competence. These are based on the work of Spivack and Shure (1974) as described in Chapter Three.

Elias and Clabby (1992) describe a multicomponent, multi-level prevention program, the Improving Social Awareness–Social Problem Solving (ISA) Project. It consists of a curriculum that provides training in social problem-solving readiness and critical thinking skills at the elementary school level. At the secondary school level, preventive efforts are targeted at specific problem areas, such as substance abuse and suicide, and school staff are taught to incorporate ISA approaches into the academic curriculum, extra-curricular activities, study and discipline procedures, and other aspects of the school structure. In addition, parents are involved as skill elicitors and home trainers.

## Summary

Coping skills training has been used as a major component of programs that focus on preventing a range of problems in children and adolescents. Positive results have been found in programs that include coping skills training to prevent alcohol and other drug abuse, pregnancy and sexually transmitted diseases, and suicide. It appears that coping skills training may also be useful in helping children and adolescents deal with the experience of disaster or trauma. In addition, this type of training has been used successfully to enhance general emotional and social competence.

# *Twelve*

---  △△  ---

# Successful Implementation

In this book, a variety of coping skills interventions have been reviewed; these interventions can be implemented in school settings
and can provide children and adolescents with constructive ways of
dealing with the variety of potential stressors that they may encounter. However, successful implementation of programs in complex
settings such as schools requires more than knowledge of the intervention procedures themselves and the evaluative literature documenting their effectiveness. The unique organizational structure
and decision-making processes of schools must be considered in
planning for implementation of coping skills interventions. This
final chapter will address issues related to the school organization
that will influence the effectiveness with which coping skills interventions are implemented.

### Approval

Approval from a variety of sources is necessary for successful implementation of coping skills interventions in school settings. These

sources include administrators, teachers, parents, and the students themselves.

If coping skills interventions are to be implemented with individual students as a means of treating an identified emotional or behavioral problem, administrative approval of and parental consent for use of the treatment approach is typically necessary, although the expertise and recommendation of the helping professional weigh heavily in the approval process. Administrative approval in a more general sense may also be necessary to validate the implementation of emotional and behavioral interventions with students as an appropriate role for the school-based helping professional. When these interventions are used with groups of students with identified problems, administrative approval and parental consent are also necessary, and building-level administrators typically want to be apprised of the objectives of and procedures used with the group so they can be assured of having adequate information about the educational programs occurring within their area of responsibility.

When coping skills interventions are used with groups of students in a prevention program, administrative approval at the building and sometimes district level is necessary as well, and the decision is typically scrutinized very carefully. At times school administrators may be reluctant to approve implementation of prevention programs because they think that such implementation will indicate to the public that their school or school district has a problem in the area targeted for preventive intervention (such as drug abuse or suicide). Forman and Linney (1988) suggest that, when requesting approval for prevention programs from 'school administrators, the program developer should be prepared to answer several questions.

First, why do we need the prevention program? National statistics and information about negative consequences of the target problem for students, particularly with respect to learning and school behavior, will help to establish the relevance and importance of the program as it affects the development of students and the goals of the school and school district.

Second, why should the specific program suggested be implemented? A nontechnical, jargon-free description of program rationale and content as well as information about effectiveness and similar programs conducted in similar school districts will establish a case for implementation.

Third, what are the costs? Information should be provided concerning materials, space, staff training, staff time, and student time needed.

Fourth, what are the benefits? The program initiator should make available information regarding the types of students who will benefit, the ways in which they will benefit, with particular emphasis on school behavior, and other ways in which the school or school district may benefit, such as through local or national recognition.

Who might oppose implementation of the intervention and how can this opposition be addressed? Resistance to implementation of preventive interventions can be addressed by involving teachers, parents, and students in content and implementation planning activities.

Parental consent for student participation in coping skills prevention programs is typically required if only some students are taken out of class for the program because they are at risk for the target problem. At times, parents may be reluctant to provide consent for participation in prevention programs because they think such participation will identify their child as having the target problem. When the prevention program is implemented as part of the regular curriculum to whole classrooms, parental consent is usually unnecessary; however, a number of researchers in this area have indicated that parental knowledge and approval of the program can be a means of enhancing program effectiveness.

When administrators and parents resist implementation of prevention programs because they fear negative publicity and identification with the target problem, they should be given extensive information about the program rationale, content, and effectiveness. The use of prevention programs to prevent problems should be underscored as a means of dealing with such concerns.

A sizable body of literature has been developed in the last ten years concerning the acceptability of behavioral and cognitive-behavioral interventions among teachers. This literature provides direction for helping professionals working in the schools and implementing coping skills training programs that require teacher assistance in their implementation. Researchers in this area agree that an individual's opinions about and evaluation of an intervention will affect whether it is implemented at all, the length of time it is implemented, and whether it is implemented appropriately.

Witt and Elliot (1985) summarized the results of research on the acceptability of behavioral interventions and generated five conclusions: (1) interventions differ in their acceptability; (2) the severity of the target behavior affects treatment acceptability, and the more severe a problem is, the more acceptable is any treatment; (3) the presence of negative side effects due to an intervention has negative effects on its acceptability; (4) positive behavioral interventions (such as positive reinforcement) are viewed as more acceptable than reductive interventions (such as time out); and (5) acceptability ratings are affected by the amount of time, effort, and resources used during implementation, with more demanding interventions receiving lower acceptability ratings.

In a more recent review of this literature, Elliott (1988) also described the effects of knowledge of treatments, past experience with treatments, and type of teacher education and training. He found some evidence that (1) positive attitudes toward behavioral techniques follow increases in knowledge of these techniques; (2) regular and special education teachers do not evaluate the acceptability of treatments differently; and (3) teachers with more experience tend to find all treatments less acceptable.

Harris, Preller, and Graham (1990) have recently extended this line of inquiry to cognitive-behavioral interventions. These investigators asked 203 teachers to evaluate two cognitive-behavioral interventions (self-instruction training and self-monitoring) and two behavioral interventions (token economy and social reinforcement). Teachers found all four interventions to be acceptable. At the mild problem level, social reinforcement and self-monitoring were significantly more acceptable than self-instruction training and a token economy. Self-instruction training was more acceptable at the severe problem level than at the mild level, and social reinforcement was more acceptable at the mild level than at the severe level. The investigators indicated that, in terms of teacher time, effort, and resources, self-instructional training was probably viewed as more intensive and costly than necessary for a mild problem. They concluded that there was evidence of the acceptability of cognitive-behavioral interventions by practicing teachers. Although further research is needed in this area, the existing literature indicates that teachers are likely to view their participation in coping skills interventions in a positive manner if their efforts are supported with appropriate resources and if the effort they expend in implementing these interventions is seen as causing a significant reduction in the problems of their students.

A small number of studies have also examined the acceptability of interventions to children. Elliott, Witt, Galvin, and Moe (1986) found that students rated private teacher-student interactions, group reinforcement, and negative sanctions for misbehaving children as most acceptable. Public reprimand and negative group contingencies were rated as unacceptable interventions. Although this line of investigation also needs to be extended to cognitive-behavioral coping skills interventions, extant literature indicates that coping skills interventions are likely to be acceptable to students because they may involve private trainer-student interactions and positive contingencies, and they do not have public negative consequences.

### Support

Approval from school administrators typically implies that the coping skills intervention will address a need, will be consistent with the philosophy and the goals of the school, and will be potentially useful in achieving those goals. In addition to approval, tangible evidence of support will be necessary for successful implementation.

Such support will include release time for teacher training if teacher participation in the intervention is necessary. If training is done during the school day, support may also include provision of substitute teachers for classes while teachers are participating in training. If training is done after school working hours, provision of a stipend for attendance may be needed. Training should be multisession and should include demonstration, structured practice, and feedback. Training sessions should be supplemented by classroom observation and feedback sessions as well as opportunities for consultation regarding accurate program implementation.

Administrative support must also address space needs and scheduling. When individuals or small groups of students participate in coping skills training interventions, adequate, comfortable space in which the sessions may be held in confidence must be provided. All efforts should be made to schedule training sessions at times when students will not miss instruction in major subjects. At the same time, the training sessions should not be scheduled so that students will miss their favorite parts of the school day. If this occurs students will be reluctant to participate and likely to approach the training with a negative attitude. Students who are taken out of classes to participate in these programs should be given the time and support needed to make up any work they may have missed. When coping skills training is provided for an entire class, the use of classroom time for this type of program must be administratively sanctioned.

Finally, adequate support for coping skills training interventions will also include funds for materials and equipment. Many of these interventions require use of training manuals, student workbooks, tangible rewards for student participation and goal attainment, and audiotapes and/or videotapes.

## Programming for Generalization and Maintenance

Generalization refers to transfer of training to settings and situations beyond those in which training was conducted. Maintenance refers to program durability or sustained behavior change after training is terminated. Attention to generalization and maintenance is essential for effective coping skills training programs and is a major factor in determining program success.

Inherent in the coping skills training approach is an emphasis on generalization and maintenance issues, as this approach is designed to provide youngsters with social and emotional skills they can use to deal with a variety of potentially stressful situations outside the training setting. A number of specific procedures have been identified in the behavioral and cognitive-behavioral literature that can be used in the design and implementation of coping skills interventions to ensure generalization and maintenance of behavior change. Some of these procedures can be carried out during coping skills training sessions; others extend to training opportunities outside the scheduled sessions.

Provision of general principles of behavior is one within-training factor that can be used to enhance generalization and maintenance. When a coping skill is presented, information concerning general principles, rules, and strategies should be given so that students will understand why and how the skill works and the range of problem situations that the skill may be used in. In addition, training in a particular coping skill should include instructions regarding how to use the skill in a variety of situations. Numerous opportunities for skill rehearsal through role-play and homework assignments will increase students' familiarity with potentially stressful situations that may be dealt with constructively through use of coping skills. Use in the training setting of discriminative stimuli that have a high probability of occurring in the posttraining environment can provide helpful cues to the trainee to utilize coping skills in these stressful situations.

Kendall and Braswell (1985) emphasize the importance of training for relapse prevention. This involves recognition that students will probably encounter some failure experiences when initially attempting to use coping skills. Therefore, training should include instruction in and practice with such experiences.

An additional within-training method of enhancing maintenance is scheduling of booster sessions. Often these are scheduled at monthly intervals, or after an event that is likely to be stressful. Booster sessions allow the student to obtain additional support regarding use of coping skills in stressful situations that have been encountered since the termination of training.

As indicated in the previous chapter on prevention applications, generalization and maintenance of behavior change resulting from coping skills training programs can be enhanced when significant others in the youngster's natural environment are trained to encourage use of coping skills outside the training situation or setting. These significant others typically include teachers and parents who can model, cue, and reinforce use of coping skills in the classroom and home setting on a daily basis (Forman & Linney,

1991). In addition, when groups of children or adolescents are trained to use coping skills, they can be instructed to encourage each other to use the skills outside the training setting, thereby taking advantage of the powerful influence that peers can have on behavior (McConnell, 1987).

## Monitoring and Evaluation

Continuous monitoring of coping skills interventions during implementation as well as evaluation after termination of training is necessary to ensure program success and to gain information concerning the types of changes that need to be made to increase effectiveness. Because of heavy workloads, helping professionals working in the schools may be tempted to overlook this important aspect of implementation, thinking that it detracts from their time serving students. However, this aspect of implementation provides the information that can be used to monitor the well-being and progress of student participants, to make adjustments in the intervention during implementation to increase effectiveness, and to assess overall program success.

Azarnoff and Seliger (1982) explain that the focus of monitoring is on the process of service delivery while the focus of evaluation is on the product or outcome rather than the process. Monitoring answers the question, Is the program being implemented appropriately and according to plan? Evaluation answers the question, Are objectives for participant change being met?

Both monitoring and evaluation must be linked directly to program planning and should be viewed as part of effective implementation. Both require that program goals and goals for individual program participants be made explicit in terms of measurable objectives. They also require identification of measurement instruments that allow for the comparison of accomplishment or performance against objectives; additionally, data sources, time intervals to be used for data collection, and methods of data analysis must be determined.

Through monitoring, accuracy of implementation in terms of participant attendance, participant adherence to program requirements, delivery of program content, and program length can be assessed. Information obtained through program monitoring may be used to explain the relationship between specific program components and program outcomes or why an intervention may have failed to reach its goals. Such information can be used for program modification during program implementation or in planning future interventions.

Through evaluation, program impact or effectiveness can be assessed. The degree to which program goals have been attained and the confidence with which change in program participants can be attributed to the intervention is examined through this process. Maher and Kratochwill (1980) suggest that in addition to conducting an outcome evaluation in which the complete intervention is evaluated, an interim progress evaluation should be conducted at specified time intervals in order to obtain information about the progress individual students are making toward attaining intervention goals.

Classical experimental research designs are typically not used in evaluation efforts in the schools; however, quasiexperimental designs, including comparative studies and time series designs, are used frequently to evaluate these interventions. In comparative studies, when random assignment is not possible, a treatment group and a control group of participants can be compared through measurements made before and after the intervention. Time series designs involve multiple measurements of participants before, during, and after the intervention; with these data, trends over time can then be examined.

Measuring participant knowledge of coping skills strategies as well as emotional and/or behavioral responses targeted for change both within and outside the training setting are essential for evaluating program outcome. When change in individual participants is evaluated, magnitude of change, breadth of change, durability of change, and presence of negative side effects should be considered. When the evaluation involves change in groups of students, the proportion of students who improve is an additional important issue for consideration.

Finally, consumer satisfaction is a significant area for consideration in the evaluation of coping skills interventions. Wolf (1978) has used the term *social validity* to refer to the evaluation of treatment by consumers. Social validity includes the acceptability of the intervention goals, the acceptability of the intervention procedures, and the social importance of the outcomes of the intervention. Reactions of students, parents, and teachers regarding satisfaction with coping skills interventions will have a major impact on whether the intervention is implemented fully to termination, and whether additional coping skills interventions are implemented in the future.

## Summary

Coping skills interventions provide a way to help children and adolescents develop a repertoire of constructive responses to a range of potential stressors. In addition to expert knowledge of and skill in these intervention procedures, the helping professional working in the schools needs to be cognizant of a number of issues that will influence the success of the implementation. These issues include the need for approval and support from a variety of sources, the requirement for specific attention to programming for generalization and maintenance, and the need to monitor and evaluate the intervention. Attention to these issues should greatly increase the probability of successful implementation and should thereby assist in enhancing the skills of children and adolescents in coping with the minor and major problem situations they encounter in their daily lives.

# References

Abramson, L. Y., Seligman, E. D., & Teasdale, J. D. (1978). Learned helplessness in humans: Critique and reformation. *Journal of Abnormal Psychology, 87,* 49-74.

Achenbach, T. M., & Edelbrock, C. (1983). *Manual for the Child Behavior Checklist and Revised Child Behavior Profile.* Burlington, VT: University of Vermont Department of Psychiatry.

Albee, G. W. (1982). Preventing psychopathology and promoting human potential. *American Psychologist, 37,* 1043-1050.

Alberti, R., & Emmons, M. (1975). *Your perfect right: A guide to assertive behavior.* San Luis Obispo, CA: IMPACT Publishers.

Allen, K. E., Hart, B., Buell, T. S., Harris, F. R., & Wolf, M. M. (1964). Effects of social reinforcement on isolate behavior of a nursery school child. *Child Development, 35,* 511-518.

Asarnow, J. R., Carlson, G. A., & Guthrie, D. (1987). Coping strategies, self-perceptions, and hopelessness, and perceived family environments in depressed and suicidal children. *Journal of Consulting and Clinical Psychology, 55,* 361-366.

Azarnoff, R. S., & Seliger, J. S. (1982). *Delivering human services.* Englewood Cliffs, NJ: Prentice-Hall.

Babouri, E. M. (1985). Use of the group modality in the prevention of sexually transmitted diseases among adolescent girls. *International Journal of Adolescent Medicine and Health, 1,* 325-336.

Ballard, K. D., & Glynn, T. (1975). Behavioral self-management in story writing with elementary school children. *Journal of Applied Behavior Analysis, 8,* 387-398.

Bandura, A. (1969). *Principles of behavior modification.* Troy, MO: Holt, Rinehart & Winston.

Barnes, L. L. (1976). The effects of relaxation and music on stabilizing recall of didactic material. *Dissertation Abstracts International, 37,* 1397-1398.

Barrera, M. (1981). Social support's role in the adjustment of pregnant adolescents: Assessment issues and findings. In B. H. Gottleib (Ed.), *Social networks and social support in community mental health* (pp. 69-96). Beverly Hills, CA: Sage.

Barton, E. J., & Ascione, F. R. (1984). Direct observation. In T. H. Ollendick & M. Hersen (Eds.), *Child behavioral assessment* (pp. 166-194). Elmsford, NY: Pergamon Press.

Bash, M.A.S., & Camp, B. W. (1980). Teacher training in the Think Aloud Classroom Program. In G. Cartledge & J. F. Milburn (Eds.), *Teaching social skills to children: Innovative approaches* (pp. 143-178). Elmsford, NY: Pergamon Press.

Beautrais, A. L., Fergusson, D. M., & Shannon, F. T. (1982). Life events and childhood morbidity: A prospective study. *Pediatrics, 70,* 935-940.

Beck, A. (1976). *Cognitive therapy and emotional disorders.* New York: International Universities Press.

Beck, A. T., Rush, A. J., Shaw, B. F., & Emery, G. (1979). *Cognitive therapy of depression.* New York: Guilford Press.

Bedell, J. R., Giordani, B., Amour, J. L., Tavormina, J., & Boll, T. (1977). Life stress and the psychological and medical adjustment of chronically ill children. *Journal of Psychosomatic Research, 21,* 237-242.

Bergland, B., & Chal, A. (1972). Relaxation training and a junior high behavior problem. *School Counselor, 19,* 288-293.

Bernard, M. E. (1979, April). *Rational-emotive group counseling in a school setting.* Paper presented at the annual meeting of the American Education Research Association, San Francisco.

Bernard, M. E. (1990). Rational-emotive therapy with children and adolescents: Treatment strategies. *School Psychology Review, 19,* 294-303.

Bernard, M. E., & Joyce, M. R. (1984). *Rational-emotive therapy with children and adolescents: Theory, treatment strategies, preventative methods.* New York: Wiley.

Bernard, M. E., & Laws, W. (1988, August). *Childhood irrationality and mental health: Development of a scale.* Paper presented at the 24th International Congress of Psychology, Sydney.

Bierman, K. L., & Furman, W. (1984). The effects of social skills training and peer involvement on the social adjustment of preadolescents. *Child Development, 55,* 151–162.

Bierman, K. L., Miller, C. L., & Stabb, S. D. (1987). Improving the social behavior and peer acceptance of rejected boys: Effects of social skill training with instructions and prohibitions. *Journal of Consulting and Clinical Psychology, 55,* 194–200.

Block, J. (1978). Effects of a rational-emotive mental health program on poorly achieving, disruptive high school students. *Journal of Counseling Psychology, 25,* 61–65.

Bolstad, O. D., & Johnson, S. M. (1972). Self-regulation in the modification of disruptive classroom behavior. *Journal of Applied Behavior Analysis, 5,* 443–454.

Borkowski, J. G., Weyhing, R. S., & Turner, L. A. (1986). Attributional retraining and the teaching of strategies. *Exceptional Children, 53,* 130–137.

Bornstein, M. R., Bellack, A. S., & Hersen, M. (1977). Social-skills training for assertive children: A multiple-baseline analysis. *Journal of Applied Behavior Analysis, 10,* 183–195.

Bornstein, P. H., & Knapp, M. (1981). Self-control desensitization with a multi-phobic boy: A multiple baseline design. *Journal of Behavior Therapy and Experimental Psychiatry, 12,* 281–285.

Botvin, G. J. (1983). *Life skills training: A self-improvement approach to substance abuse prevention.* New York: Smithfield Press.

Botvin, G. J. (1987). *Factors inhibiting drug use: Teacher and peer effects.* Report presented to the National Institute on Drug Abuse, Rockville, MD.

Botvin, G. J. (1989). *Life skills training: Teacher's manual.* New York: Smithfield Press.

Botvin, G. J., Baker, E., Renick, N., Filazzola, A. D., & Botvin, E. M. (1984). A cognitive-behavioral approach to substance abuse prevention. *Addictive Behaviors, 9,* 137–147.

Botvin, G., & Eng, A. (1982). The efficacy of a multi-component approach to the prevention of cigarette smoking. *Preventive Medicine, 11,* 199–211.

Botvin, G., Eng, A., & Williams, C. (1980). Preventing the onset of smoking through life skills training. *Preventive Medicine, 9,* 135–143.

Botvin, G., Renick, N., & Baker, E. (1983, November). *Life skills training and smoking prevention: A one year follow-up.* Paper presented at the annual meeting of the American Public Health Association, Los Angeles, CA.

Botvin, G., & Wills, J. (1985). Personal and social skills training: Cognitive-behavioral approaches to substance abuse prevention. *National Institute on Drug Abuse Monographs, 63,* 8–49.

Boyce, T. W., Jensen, E. W., Cassell, J. C., Collier, A. M., Smith, A. H., & Raimey, C. T. (1973). Influence of life events and family routines on childhood respiratory tract illness. *Pediatrics, 60,* 609–615.

Brand, A. H., Johnson, J. H., & Johnson, S. B. (1986). *The relationship between life stress and diabetic control in insulin-dependent diabetic children and adolescents.* Unpublished manuscript, University of Florida.

Braud, L. W. (1978). The effects of frontal EMG biofeedback and progressive relaxation upon hyperactivity and its behavioral concomitants. *Biofeedback and Self-Regulation, 3,* 69–89.

Brigham, T. A. (1989). *Self-management for adolescents: A skills-training program.* New York: Guilford.

Brigham, T. A., Contreras, J. A., Handel, G. S., & Castillo, A. O. (1983). A comparison of two approaches for improving social and job placement skills. *Behavioral Engineering, 8,* 104–115.

Brigham, T. A., Hopper, C., Hill, B., de Armas, A., & Newsom, P. (1985). A self-management program for disruptive adolescents in the school: A clinical replication analysis. *Behavior Therapy, 16,* 99–115.

Broden, M., Hall, R. V., & Mitts, B. (1971). The effects of self-recording on the classroom behavior of two eighth-grade students. *Journal of Applied Behavior Analysis, 4,* 191–200.

Brooks-Gunn, J., Boyer, C. B., & Hein, K. (1988). Preventing HIV infection and AIDS in children and adolescents: Behavioral research and intervention strategies. *American Psychologist, 43,* 958–964.

Brown, D. P. (1977). A model for the levels of concentrative meditation. *International Journal of Clinical and Experimental Hypnosis, 24,* 236–273.

Bruno-Golden, B. F. (1978). Relaxation training used to enhance listening skills and productive oral comprehension for a language delayed child. *Dissertation Abstracts International, 39,* 2824.

Camp, B. W. (1980). Two psycho-educational treatment programs for young aggressive boys. In C. K. Whalen & B. Henkler (Eds.), *Hyperactive children: The social psychology of intervention of children and adults* (pp. 191–219). Elmsford, NY: Pergamon.

Camp, B. W., & Bash, M. A. (1980). Think aloud: Improving self-control through training in problem-solving. In D. P. Rathjen & J. P. Foreyt (Eds.), *Social competence: Intervention for children and adults* (pp. 24–53). Elmsford, NY: Pergamon.

Camp, B. W., Blom, G., Hebert, F., & van Doorninck, W. (1977). "Think Aloud": A program for developing self-control in young aggressive boys. *Journal of Abnormal Child Psychology, 5,* 157–168.

Carter, J. L., & Synolds, D. (1974). Effects of relaxation training upon handwriting quality. *Journal of Learning Disabilities, 7,* 53–55.

Cartledge, G., & Milburn, J. F. (1978). The case for teaching social skills in the classroom: A review. *Review of Educational Research, 1,* 133–156.

Cartledge, G., & Milburn, J. F. (Eds.). (1980). *Teaching skills to children: Innovative approaches.* Elmsford, NY: Pergamon.

Cautela, J. R. (1971). Covert conditioning. In A. Jacobs & L. B. Sachs (Eds.), *The psychology of private events: Perspectives on covert response systems* (pp. 112–130). San Diego, CA: Academic Press.

Cautela, J. R., & Groden, J. (1978). *Relaxation: A comprehensive manual for adults, children, and children with special needs.* Champaign, IL: Research Press.

Cecil, M. A., & Forman, S. G. (1990). Effects of stress inoculation training and coworker support groups on teachers' stress. *Journal of School Psychology, 28,* 105–118.

Cecil, M. A., & Medway, F. J. (1986). Attribution retraining with low-achieving and learned helpless children. *Techniques: A Journal for Remedial Education and Counseling, 2,* 173–181.

Chapin, M., & Dyck, G. (1976). Persistence in children's reading behavior as a function of N length and attribution retraining. *Journal of Abnormal Psychology, 85,* 511–515.

Chase, H. P., & Jackson, G. G. (1981). Stress and sugar control in children with insulin-dependent diabetes mellitus. *Journal of Pediatrics, 98,* 1011–1013.

Children's Defense Fund. (1987). *Opportunities for prevention: Building after-school and summer programs for young adolescents.* Washington, DC: Adolescent Pregnancy Prevention Clearinghouse.

Chittenden, G. E. (1942). An experimental study in measuring and modifying assertive behavior in young children. *Monographs of the Society for Research in Child Development, 7*(1, Serial No. 31).

Coddington, R. D. (1972a). The significance of life events as etiologic factors in the diseases of children. I. A survey of professionals. *Journal of Psychosomatic Research, 16,* 7–18.

Coddington, R. D. (1972b). The significance of life events as etiologic factors in the diseases of children. II. A study of a normal population. *Journal of Psychosomatic Research, 16,* 205–213.

Coddington, R. D., & Troxell, J. R. (1980). The effect of emotional factors on football injury rates: A pilot study. *Journal of Human Stress, 6,* 3–5.

Cohen-Sandler, R., Berman, A. L., & King, R. A. (1982). Life stress and symptomatology. Determinants of suicidal behavior in children. *Journal of the American Academy of Child Psychiatry, 21,* 178–186.

Combs, M. L., & Slaby, D. A. (1978). Social-skills training with children. In B. Lahey & A. Kazdin (Eds.), *Advances in clinical child psychology* (Vol. 1, pp. 161–201). New York: Plenum.

Compas, B. E. (1987a). Stress and life events during childhood and adolescence. *Clinical Psychology Review, 7,* 275–302.

Compas, B. E. (1987b). Coping with stress during childhood and adolescence. *Psychological Bulletin, 101,* 393–403.

Compas, B. E., Davis, G. E., & Forsythe, C. J. (1985). Characteristics of life events during adolescence. *American Journal of Community Psychology, 13,* 677–691.

Compas, B. E., Davis, G. E., Forsythe, C. J., & Wagner, B. M. (1987). Assessment of major and daily stressful events during adolescence: The Adolescent Perceived Events Scale. *Journal of Consulting and Clinical Psychology, 55,* 534–541.

Compas, B. E., Malcarne, V. L., & Fondacaro, K. M. (1988). Coping with stressful events in older children and young adolescents. *Journal of Consulting and Clinical Psychology, 56,* 405–411.

Connor, J., Dann, L., & Twentyman, C. (1982). A self-report measure of assertiveness in young adolescents. *Journal of Clinical Psychology, 38,* 101–106.

Cooke, T. P., & Apolloni, T. (1976). Developing positive social-emotional behaviors: A study of training and generalization effects. *Journal of Applied Behavior Analysis, 9,* 65–78.

Copeland, A. P. (1981). The relevance of subject variables in cognitive self-instructional programs for impulsive children. *Behavior Therapy, 12,* 520–529.

Cowen, E. L., Weissberg, R. P., & Guare, J. (1984). Differentiating attributes of children referred to a school mental health program. *Journal of Abnormal Child Psychology, 12,* 397–410.

Crandall, V. C., Katkovsky, W., & Crandall, V. J. (1965). Children's belief in their own control of reinforcements in intellectual-academic situations. *Child Development, 36,* 91–109.

Davis, J. M., & Sandoval, J. (1991). *Suicidal youth: School-based intervention and prevention.* San Francisco: Jossey-Bass.

Davis, J. M., Sandoval, J., & Wilson, M. P. (1988). Strategies for the primary prevention of adolescent suicide. *School Psychology Review, 17,* 559–569.

DeCharms, R. (1972). Personal causation training in the schools. *Journal of Applied Social Psychology, 2,* 95–113.

Del Greco, L., Breitbach, L., Rumer, S., McCarthy, R. H., & Suissa, S. (1986). Four-year results of a youth smoking prevention program using assertiveness training. *Adolescence, 21,* 631–640.

Diener, C., & Dweck, C. S. (1978). An analysis of learned helplessness: Continuous changes in performance, strategy, and achievement cognitions following failure. *Journal of Personality and Social Psychology, 36,* 451–462.

DiGuiseppe, R. A. (1981). Cognitive therapy with children. In G. Emery, S. D. Hollon, & R. C. Bedrosian (Eds.), *New directions in cognitive therapy.* New York: Guilford.

DiGiuseppe, R. A., & Kassinove, H. (1976). Effects of a rational-emotive school mental health program on children's emotional adjustment. *Journal of Community Psychology, 4,* 382–387.

DiNardo, P. A., & DiNardo, P. G. (1981). Self-control desensitization in the treatment of a childhood phobia. *The Behavior Therapist, 4,* 15–16.

Douglas, V. I., Parry, P., Marton, P., & Garson, C. (1976). Assessment of a cognitive training program for hyperactive children. *Journal of Abnormal Child Psychology, 4,* 389–410.

Dush, D. M., Hirt, M. L., & Schroeder, H. E. (1989). Self-statement modification in the treatment of child behavior disorders: A meta-analysis. *Psychological Bulletin, 106,* 97–106.

Dweck, C. S. (1975). The role of expectations and attributions in the alleviation of learned helplessness. *Journal of Personality and Social Psychology, 31,* 674–685.

D'Zurilla, T., & Goldfried, M. (1971). Problem solving and behavior modification. *Journal of Abnormal Psychology, 78,* 107–129.

Eisler, R. M., Miller, P. M., & Hersen, M. (1973). Components of assertive behavior. *Journal of Clinical Psychology, 24,* 295–299.

Elardo, P. T., & Caldwell, B. M. (1979). The effects of an experimental social development program on children in the middle childhood period. *Psychology in the Schools, 16,* 93–100.

Elias, M. J., & Branden, L. R. (1988). Primary prevention of behavioral and emotional problems in school-aged populations. *School Psychology Review, 17,* 581–592.

Elias, M. J., & Clabby, J. F. (1992). *Building social problem-solving skills: Guidelines from a school-based program.* San Francisco: Jossey-Bass.

Elias, M. J., Gara, M., Ubriaco, M., Rothbaum, D. A., Clabby, J. F., & Schuyler, T. (1986). Impact of a preventive social problem solving intervention on children's coping with middle-school stressors. *American Journal of Community Psychology, 14,* 259–275.

Elitzer, B. (1976). Self-relaxation programs for acting out adolescents. *Adolescence, 44,* 570–572.

Elliott, S. N. (1988). Acceptability of behavioral treatments: Review of variables that influence treatment selection. *Professional Psychology: Research and Practice, 19,* 68–80.

Elliott, S. N., Gresham, F. M., & Heffer, R. W. (1987). Social skills interventions. In C. A. Maher & J. Zins (Eds.), *Psychoeducational interventions in schools* (pp. 141–159). Elmsford, NY: Pergamon.

Elliott, S. N., Sheridan, S. M., & Gresham, F. M. (1989). Assessing and treating social skills deficits: A case study for the scientist-practitioner. *Journal of School Psychology, 27,* 197–222.

Elliott, S. N., Witt, J. C., Galvin, G. A., & Moe, G. L. (1986). Children's involvement in intervention selection: Acceptability of interventions for misbehaving peers. *Professional Psychology: Research and Practice, 17,* 235–241.

Ellis, A. (1977). The basic clinical theory of rational-emotive therapy. In A. Ellis & R. Grieger (Eds.), *Handbook of rational-emotive therapy* (pp. 3–34). New York: Springer.

Ellis, A. (1980). An overview of the clinical theory of rational-emotive therapy. In R. Grieger & J. Boyd (Eds.), *Rational-emotive therapy: A skills-based approach* (pp. 1–31). New York: Van Nostrand Reinhold.

Ellis, A., & Bernard, M. E. (Eds.). (1983). *Rational-emotive approaches to the problems of childhood.* New York: Plenum Press.

Epstein, S. (1967). Toward a unified theory of anxiety. In B. Maher (Ed.), *Progress in experimental personality* (Vol. 4, pp. 1–89). San Diego, CA: Academic Press.

Evans, R. I. (1976). Smoking in children: Developing a social psychological strategy of deterrence. *Journal of Preventive Medicine, 5,* 122–127.

Evers-Pasquale, W., & Sherman, M. (1975). The reward value of peers. *Journal of Abnormal Child Psychology, 3,* 179–189.

Ewart, C. K., Harris, W. L., Iwata, M. M., Coates, T. J., Bullock, R., & Simon, B. (1987). Feasibility and effectiveness of school-based relaxation in lowering blood pressure. *Health Psychology, 6,* 399–416.

Feindler, E. L., Marriott, S. A., & Iwata, M. (1984). Group anger control training for junior high school delinquents. *Cognitive Therapy and Research, 8,* 299-311.

Flay, B. R., d'Avernas, J. R., Best, J. A., Kersell, M. W., & Ryan, K. B. (1983). Cigarette smoking: Why young people do it and ways of preventing it. In P. J. McGrath & P. Firestove (Eds.), *Pediatric and behavioral medicine* (pp. 132-183). New York: Springer.

Folkman, S., & Lazarus, R. S. (1980). An analysis of coping in a middle-aged sample. *Journal of Health and Social Behavior, 21,* 219-239.

Fontana, A., & Dovidio, J. F. (1984). The relationship between stressful life events and school related performances of Type A and Type B adolescents. *Journal of Human Stress, 10,* 50-54.

Forman, S. G. (1982). Stress management for teachers: A cognitive-behavioral program. *Journal of School Psychology, 30,* 180-187.

Forman, S. G. (1983). Cognitive-behavioral approaches to management of occupational stress. *Child and Youth Services Review, 5,* 277-287.

Forman, S. G., & Linney, J. A. (1988). School-based prevention of adolescent substance abuse: Programs, implementation and future directions. *School Psychology Review, 17,* 550-558.

Forman, S. G., & Linney, J. A. (1991). School-based social and personal coping skills training. In L. Donohew, H. E. Sypher, & W. J. Bukoski (Eds.), *Persuasive communication and drug abuse prevention* (pp. 263-282). Hillsdale, NJ: Erlbaum.

Forman, S. G., & O'Malley, P. L. (1984). School stress and anxiety interventions. *School Psychology Review, 13,* 162-170.

Forman, S. G., & O'Malley, P. L. (1985). School-based approach to stress management education of students. *Special Services in the Schools, 1,* 61-71.

Foster, S. L., & Ritchey, W. L. (1979). Issues in the assessment of social competence in children. *Journal of Applied Behavior Analysis, 12,* 625-638.

Fowler, J. W., & Peterson, P. L. (1981). Increasing reading persistence and altering attributional style of learned helpless children. *Journal of Educational Psychology, 73,* 251-260.

Frederiksen, L. W., & Frederiksen, C. B. (1975). Teacher-determined and self-determined token reinforcement in a special education classroom. *Behavior Therapy, 6,* 310–314.

Gad, M. T., & Johnson, J. H. (1980). Correlates of adolescent life stress as related to race, sex and levels of perceived social support. *Journal of Clinical Child Psychology, 9,* 13–16.

Gerler, E. R., & Danielson, H. A. (1984). The quieting reflex and success imagery. *Elementary School Guidance and Counseling, 19,* 152–155.

Gesten, E. L., & Weissberg, R. P. (1986). Social problem-solving training with children: A guide to effective practice. *Special Services in the Schools, 2,* 19–39.

Gist, R., & Lubin, B. (Eds.). (1989). *Psychosocial aspects of disaster.* New York: Wiley.

Glynn, E. L. (1970). Classroom applications of self-determined reinforcement. *Journal of Applied Behavior Analysis, 3,* 123–132.

Glynn, E. L., & Thomas, J. D. (1974). Effect of cuing on self-control of classroom behavior. *Journal of Applied Behavior Analysis, 7,* 299–306.

Glynn, E. L., Thomas, J. D., & Shee, S. M. (1973). Behavioral self-control of on-task behavior in an elementary classroom. *Journal of Applied Behavior Analysis, 6,* 105–113.

Goldfried, M., Decenteceo, E., & Weinberg, L. (1974). Systematic rational restructuring as a self-control technique. *Behavior Therapy, 5,* 247–254.

Goldstein, A. P., Sherman, M., Gershaw, N. J., Sprafkin, R. P., & Glick, B. (1978). Training aggressive adolescents in prosocial behavior. *Journal of Youth and Adolescence, 7,* 73–92.

Goldstein, A. P., Sprafkin, R. P., & Gershaw, N. J. (1976). *Skill training for community living.* Elmsford, NY: Pergamon.

Goldstein, A. P., Sprafkin, R. P., Gershaw, N. J., & Klein, P. (1980). *Skillstreaming the adolescent: A structured learning approach to teaching prosocial skills.* Champaign, IL: Research Press.

Gottman, J. M., & McFall, R. M. (1972). Self-monitoring effects in a program for potential high school dropouts: A time series analysis. *Journal of Consulting and Clinical Psychology, 39,* 273–281.

Grant, A. E. (1980). *The effects of relaxation training on the test anxiety of public school students in grades nine through twelve.* Unpublished doctoral dissertation, University of South Carolina.

Greene, J. W., Walker, L. S., Hickson, G., & Thompson, J. (1985). Stressful life events and somatic complaints in adolescents. *Pediatrics, 75,* 19–22.

Greenleaf, D. O. (1982). The use of structured learning therapy and transfer programming with disruptive adolescents in a school setting. *Journal of School Psychology, 20,* 122–130.

Gresham, F. M., & Elliott, S. N. (1987). The relationship between adaptive behavior and social skills. *Journal of Special Education, 21,* 167–182.

Gross, A. M., Brigham, T. A., Hopper, R., & Bologna, N. C. (1980). Self-management and social skills training: A study with predelinquent and delinquent youth. *Criminal Justice and Behavior, 7,* 161–184.

Gross, A. M., & Drabman, R. S. (1982). Teaching self-recording, self-evaluation, and self-reward to nonclinic children and adolescents. In P. Karoly & F. H. Kanfer (Eds.), *Self management and behavior change from theory to practice* (pp. 285–314). Elmsford, NY: Pergamon.

Gumaer, J., & Voorneveld, R. (1975). Affective education with gifted children. *Elementary School Guidance and Counseling, 10,* 86–94.

Hajzler, D. J., & Bernard, M. E. (1991). Review of rational-emotive education outcome studies. *School Psychology Quarterly, 6,* 27–49.

Hallahan, D. P., Lloyd, J., Kosiewicz, M. M., Kauffman, J. M., & Graves, A. W. (1979). Self-monitoring of attention as a treatment for learning disabled boys' off-task behavior. *Learning Disability Quarterly, 2,* 24–32.

Harris, K. R., Preller, D. M., & Graham, S. (1990). Acceptability of cognitive-behavioral and behavioral interventions among teachers. *Cognitive Therapy and Research, 14,* 573–587.

Hart, B. M., Reynolds, N. J., Baer, D. M., Brawley, E. R., & Harris, F. R. (1968). Effect of contingent and non-contingent social reinforcement on the cooperative play of a preschool child. *Journal of Applied Behavior Analysis, 1,* 73–76.

Harter, S. (1985). *Manual for the self-perception profile for children.* Denver, CO: University of Denver Press.

Harvey, J., Ickes, W., & Kidd, R. F. (Eds.). (1978). *New directions in attribution research* (Vol. 2). Hillsdale, NJ: Erlbaum.

Heider, F. (1958). *The psychology of interpersonal relations.* New York: Wiley.

Heisel, J. S., Ream, S., Raitz, R., Rappaport, M., & Coddington, R. D. (1973). The significance of life events as contributing factors in the diseases of children. *Behavioral Pediatrics, 83,* 119–123.

Hodges, K., Kline, J. J., Barbero, G., & Flanery, R. (1984). Life events occurring in families of children with recurrent abdominal pain. *Journal of Psychosomatic Research, 28,* 185–188.

Holmes, T. H., & Rahe, R. H. (1967). The social readjustment rating scale. *Journal of Psychosomatic Research, 11,* 213–218.

Horan, J. J., & Williams, J. M. (1982). Longitudinal study of assertion training as a drug abuse prevention strategy. *American Educational Research Journal, 19,* 341–357.

Howard, M. (1983). *Postponing sexual involvement: An educational series for young teens.* Atlanta, GA: Emory Grady Teen Services Program, Grady Memorial Hospital.

Huey, W. C. (1983). Reducing adolescent aggression through group assertive training. *The School Counselor, 30,* 193–203.

Huey, W. C., & Rank, R. C. (1984). Effects of counselor and peer-led groups' assertive training on black adolescent aggression. *Journal of Counseling Psychology, 31,* 95–98.

Hughes, J. N. (1988). *Cognitive behavior therapy with children in schools.* Elmsford, NY: Pergamon.

Humphrey, L. L., Karoly, P., & Kirschenbaum, D. S. (1978). Self-management in the classroom: Self-imposed response cost versus self-reward. *Behavior Therapy, 9,* 592–601.

Jackson, K., & Hughes, H. (1978). Effects of relaxation training on cursive handwriting of fourth grade students. *Perceptual and Motor Skills, 47,* 707–712.

Jackson, K. A., Jolly, V., & Hamilton, B. (1980). Comparisons of remedial treatments for cursive handwriting of fourth-grade students. *Perceptual and Motor Skills, 51,* 1215–1221.

Jacobs, T. J., & Charles, E. (1980). Life events and the occurrence of cancer in children. *Psychosomatic Medicine, 42,* 11–24.

Jacobson, E. (1938). *Progressive relaxation.* Chicago: University of Chicago Press.

Jahoda, M. (1958). *Current concepts of positive mental health.* New York: Basic Books.

Jakibchuk, Z., & Smeriglio, V. (1976). The influence of symbolic modeling on the social behavior of preschool children with low levels of social responsiveness. *Child Development, 47,* 838–841.

Jay, S. M., Ozolins, M., Elliott, C. H., and Caldwell, S. (1983). Assessment of children's distress during painful medical procedures. *Health Psychology, 2,* 133–147.

Johnson, J. H. (1986). *Life events as stressors in childhood and adolescence.* Newbury Park, CA: Sage.

Johnson, J. H., & McCutcheon, S. (1980). Assessing life events in older children and adolescents: Preliminary findings with the life events checklist. In I. G. Sarason & C. D. Spielberger (Eds.), *Stress and anxiety* (Vol. 7, pp. 111–125). Washington, DC: Hemisphere.

Joyce, M. R. (1990). Rational-emotive parent consultation. *School Psychology Review, 19,* 304–314.

Kagan, J. (1966). Reflection-impulsivity: The generality and dynamics of conceptual tempo. *Journal of Abnormal Psychology, 71,* 17–24.

Kagan, J. (1983). Stress and coping in early development. In N. Garmezy & M. Rutter (Eds.), *Stress, coping and development in children* (pp. 191–216). New York: McGraw-Hill.

Kahn, A. U. (1989). Heterogeneity of suicidal adolescents. In S. Chess, A. Thomas, & H. E. Hertzig (Eds.), *Annual progress in child psychiatry and child development* (pp. 675–686). New York: Bruner/Mazel.

Kanfer, F. H. (1970). Self-monitoring: Methodological limitations and clinical applications. *Journal of Consulting and Clinical Psychology, 35,* 148–152.

Kanfer, F. H., & Karoly, P. (1982). *Self management and behavior change from theory to practice.* Elmsford, NY: Pergamon.

Kanfer, F. H., & Phillips, J. S. (1970). *Learning foundations of behavior therapy.* New York: Wiley.

Kapadia, E. S., & Fantuzzo, J. W. (1988). Effects of teacher and self-administered procedures on the spelling performance of learning-handicapped children. *Journal of School Psychology, 26,* 49–58.

Kassinove, H., Crisci, R., & Tiegerman, S. (1977). Developmental trends in rational thinking: Implications for rational-emotive school mental health programs. *Journal of Community Psychology, 5,* 266–274.

Kendall, P. C., & Braswell, L. (1982). Cognitive-behavioral self-control therapy for children: A components analysis. *Journal of Consulting and Clinical Psychology, 50,* 672–689.

Kendall, P. C., & Braswell, L. (1985). *Cognitive-behavioral therapy for impulsive children.* New York: Guilford.

Kendall, P. C., & Fischler, G. L. (1984). Behavioral and adjustment correlates of problem solving: Validational analyses of interpersonal cognitive problem-solving measures. *Child Development, 55,* 879–892.

Kendall, P. C., & Wilcox, L. E. (1979). Self-control in children: Development of a rating scale. *Journal of Consulting and Clinical Psychology, 47,* 1020–1029.

Kendall, P. C., & Wilcox, L. E. (1980). A cognitive-behavioral treatment for impulsivity: Concrete versus conceptual training in non-self-controlled problem children. *Journal of Consulting and Clinical Psychology, 48,* 80–91.

Kendall, P. C., & Zupan, B. A. (1981). Individual versus group application of cognitive-behavioral strategies for developing self-control in children. *Behavior Therapy, 12,* 344–359.

Klein, S. A., & Deffenbacher, J. L. (1977). Relaxation and exercise for hyperactive impulsive children. *Perceptual and Motor Skills, 45,* 1159–1162.

Knaus, W. J. (1974). *Rational emotive education: A manual for elementary school teachers.* New York: Institute for Rational Living.

Kochendofer, S. A., & Culp, D. (1979). Relaxation group: Intake procedure. *Elementary School Guidance and Counseling, 14,* 124.

Koeppen, A. S. (1974). Relaxation training for children. *Elementary School Guidance and Counseling, 9,* 14–21.

Ladd, G. W. (1981). Effectiveness of a social learning method for enhancing children's social interaction and peer acceptance. *Child Development, 52,* 171–178.

Ladd, G. W. (1984). Social skill training with children: Issues in research and practice. *Clinical Psychology Review, 4,* 317–337.

Lange, A., & Jakubowski, P. (1979). *Responsible assertive behavior.* Champaign, IL: Research Press.

Lawrence, D. B., & Russ, S. W. (1985). *Mediating variables between life stress and symptoms among young adolescents.* Paper presented at the annual meeting of the American Psychological Association, Los Angeles.

Lazarus, R. S. (1966). *Psychological stress and the coping process.* New York: McGraw-Hill.

Lazarus, R. S., & Folkman, S. (1984). *Stress, appraisal and coping.* New York: Springer.

Lazarus, R. S., & Launier, R. (1978). Stress-related transactions between persons and environment. In L. A. Pervin & M. Lewis (Eds.), *Perspectives in interactional psychology* (pp. 287–327). New York: Plenum.

Leaverton, D. R., White, C. A., McCormick, C. R., Smith, P., & Sheikholislam, B. (1980). Parental loss antecedent to childhood diabetes mellitus. *Journal of the American Academy of Child Psychiatry, 19,* 678–689.

Levesque, M. J., & Lowe, C. H. (1992). Importance of attributions and expectations in understanding academic behavior. In F. J. Medway & T. P. Cafferty (Eds.), *School psychology: A social psychological perspective* (pp. 47–81). Hillsdale, NJ: Erlbaum.

Licht, B. G. (1983). Cognitive-motivational factors that contribute to the achievement of learning disabled children. *Journal of Learning Disabilities, 16,* 483–490.

Little, S., & Jackson, B. (1974). The treatment of test anxiety through attentional and relaxation training. *Psychotherapy: Theory, Research and Practice, 11,* 175–178.

Lochman, J. E., Burch, P. R., Curry, J. F., & Lampron, L. B. (1984). Treatment and generalization effects of cognitive behavioral and goal setting interventions with aggressive boys. *Journal of Consulting and Clinical Psychology, 52,* 915–916.

Lochman, J. E., & Lampron, L. B. (1986). Situational social problem-solving skills and self-esteem of aggressive and nonaggressive boys. *Journal of Abnormal Child Psychology, 14,* 605–617.

Lochman, J. E., Nelson, W. M., & Sims, J. P. (1981). A cognitive behavioral program for use with aggressive children. *Journal of Clinical Child Psychology, 10,* 146–148.

Longshore, D. (1990). AIDS education for three high-risk populations. *Evaluation and Program Planning, 13,* 67–72.

Lorion, R. P., & Work, W. C. (1987). Affective and social skills development: Preventive strategies for a holistic approach to education. In S. G. Forman (Ed.), *School-based affective and social interventions* (pp. 155–169). New York: Haworth.

Lovitt, T. C., & Curtiss, K. (1969). Academic response rate as a function of teacher and self imposed contingencies. *Journal of Applied Behavior Analysis, 2,* 49–53.

Luchow, J. P., Crowe, T. K., & Kahn, J. P. (1985). Learned helplessness: Perceived effects of ability and effort on academic performance among EH and LD/EH children. *Journal of Learning Disabilities, 18,* 470–474.

Lupin, M., Braud, L. W., Braud, W., & Duer, W. F. (1976). Children, parents, and relaxation tapes. *Academic Therapy, 12,* 105–113.

Luria, A. R. (1961). *The role of speech in the regulation of normal and abnormal behavior.* New York: Liveright.

Mace, F. C., & Shea, M. (1990). Behavioral self-management with at risk children. *Special Services in the Schools, 6* 43–64.

Maher, C. A., & Kratochwill, T. R. (1980). Principles and procedures of program evaluation: An overview. *School Psychology Monograph, 4,* 1–24.

Matson, J. L., Rotatori, A. F., & Helsel, W. J. (1983). Development of a rating scale to measure social skills in children: The Matson Evaluation of Social Skills with Youngsters (MESSY). *Behavior Research and Therapy, 21,* 335–340.

Maultsby, M. C. (1975). Rational behavior therapy for acting-out adolescents. *Social Casework, 56,* 35–43.

McBrien, R. J. (1978). Using relaxation methods with first-grade boys. *Elementary School Guidance and Counseling, 12,* 146–152.

McCullough, J., Huntsinger, G., & May, W. (1977). Self-control treatment of aggression in a 16 year old male: Case study. *Journal of Consulting and Clinical Psychology, 45,* 322–331.

McConnell, S. R. (1987). Entrapment effects and the generalization and maintenance of social skills training for elementary school students with behavioral disorders. *Behavioral Disorders, 12,* 252–263.

McFall, R. M. (1976). Behavioral training: A skill-acquisition approach to clinical problems. In J. R. Spence, R. C. Carson, & J. W. Thibaut (Eds.), *Behavioral approaches to therapy* (pp. 227–260). Morristown, NJ: General Learning Press.

Mead, R. J. (1976). The effects of relaxation training on the attitudes and anxiety level of 9th grade potential dropouts. *Dissertation Abstracts International, 37,* 5612.

Meade, J. (1988, April). What parents should know when AIDS comes to school. *Children,* pp. 59–65.

Meichenbaum, D. (1977). *Cognitive-behavior modification: An integrative approach.* New York: Plenum.

Meichenbaum, D. (1979). Teaching children self-control. In B. B. Lahey & A. E. Kazdin (Eds.), *Advances in clinical child psychology* (Vol. 2, pp. 1–33). New York: Plenum.

Meichenbaum, D. (1985). *Stress inoculation training.* Elmsford, NY: Pergamon.

Meichenbaum, D., & Cameron, R. (1972). *Stress inoculation: A skills training approach to anxiety management.* Unpublished manuscript, University of Waterloo.

Meichenbaum, D. H., & Goodman, J. (1971). Training impulsive children to talk to themselves. *Journal of Abnormal Psychology, 77,* 115–126.

Meisels, L. (1976). Muscle relaxation as a competing self-control response for tense behavior in a young child. *Dissertation Abstracts International, 37,* 978.

Melamed, B., & Siegel, L. (1975). Reduction of anxiety in children facing hospitalization and surgery by use of filmed modeling. *Journal of Consulting and Clinical Psychology, 43,* 511–521.

Meyer, R. J., & Haggerty, R. J. (1962). Streptococcal infections in families. *Pediatrics, 29,* 539–549.

Michelson, L., Sugai, D. P., Wood, R. P., & Kazdin, A. (1983). *Social skills assessment and training with children: An empirically based handbook.* New York: Plenum.

Michelson, L., & Wood, R. (1982). Development and psychometric properties of the Children's Assertive Behavior Scale. *Journal of Behavioral Assessment, 4*, 3–14.

Miller, N. E., & Dollard, J. (1941). *Social learning and imitation.* London: Oxford University Press.

Morris, R. J., & Kratochwill, T. R. (1983). *Treating children's fears and phobias: A behavioral approach.* Elmsford, NY: Pergamon.

National Institute on Drug Abuse. (1991, Spring). Trends in drug use by high school seniors. *NIDA Notes*, p. 35.

Nelson, R. O. (1977). Assessment and function of self-monitoring. In M. Hersen, R. M. Eisler, & P. M. Miller (Eds.), *Progress in behavior modification* (Vol. 5, pp. 123–155). Elmsford, NY: Pergamon.

Nelson, W., & Birkimer, J. C. (1978). Role of self-instruction and self-reinforcement in the modification of impulsivity. *Journal of Consulting and Clinical Psychology, 46*, 183.

Nisbett, R. E., & Schachter, S. (1966). Cognitive manipulation of pain. *Journal of Experimental Social Psychology, 2*, 227–236.

Novaco, R. (1977). A stress-inoculation approach to anger management in the training of law enforcement officers. *American Journal of Community Psychology, 5*, 327–346.

O'Connor, R. D. (1969). Modification of social withdrawal through symbolic modeling. *Journal of Applied Behavior Analysis, 2*, 15–22.

O'Connor, R. D. (1972). Relative efficacy of modeling, shaping, and the combined procedures for modification of social withdrawal. *Journal of Abnormal Psychology, 79*, 327–334.

Oden, S., & Asher, S. R. (1977). Coaching children in social skills for friendship making. *Child Development, 48*, 495–506.

Ollendick, T. H. (1979). Behavioral treatment of anorexia nervosa: A five year study. *Behavior Modification, 3*, 124–135.

Ollendick, T. H., & Cerny, J. (1981). *Clinical behavior therapy with children.* New York: Plenum.

Ollendick, T. H., & Hersen, M. (1979). Social skills training for juvenile delinquents. *Behavior Research and Therapy, 17*, 547–554.

Orne, M. (1965). Psychological factors maximizing resistance to stress with special reference to hypnosis. In S. Klausner (Ed.), *The quest for self-control* (pp. 286–328). New York: Free Press.

Padawer, D. D. (1977). Reading performance of relaxation trained children. *Dissertation Abstracts International, 38,* 1306.

Padilla, E. R., Rohsenow, D. J., & Bergman, A. B. (1976). Predicting accident frequency in children. *Pediatrics, 58,* 223–226.

Paget, K. D. (1988). Adolescent pregnancy: Implications for prevention strategies in educational settings. *School Psychology Review, 17,* 570–580.

Pantell, R. H., & Goodman, B. W. (1983). Adolescent chest pain: A prospective study. *Pediatrics, 71,* 881–886.

Patterson, J. M., & McCubbin, H. I. (1983). The impact of family life events and changes on the health of a chronically ill child: Family relations. *Journal of Applied Family and Child Studies, 32,* 255–264.

Patton, P. L. (1985). A model for teaching rational behavior skills to emotionally disturbed youth in a public school setting. *The School Counselor, 32,* 381–387.

Pearlin, L. I., & Schooler, C. (1978). The structure of coping. *Journal of Health and Social Behavior, 22,* 337–356.

Pellegrini, D. S., & Urbain, E. S. (1985). An evaluation of cognitive problem-solving training with children. *Journal of Child Psychology and Psychiatry, 26,* 17–41.

Pentz, M. A. (1980). Assertiveness training and trainer effects on unassertive and aggressive adolescents. *Journal of Counseling Psychology, 27,* 70–72.

Pentz, M. A. (1985). Social competence skills and self efficacy as determinants of substance use in adolescence. In S. Shiffman & T. A. Willis (Eds.), *Coping and substance use* (pp. 117–142). New York: Academic Press.

Perry, M. A., & Furukawa, M. J. (1980). Modeling methods. In F. H. Kanfer & A. P. Goldstein (Eds.), *Helping people change* (2nd ed., pp. 131–171). Elmsford, NY: Pergamon.

Peterson, C. (1992). Learned helplessness and school problems. In F. J. Medway & T. P. Cafferty (Eds.), *School psychology: A social psychological perspective* (pp. 359–376). Hillsdale, NJ: Erlbaum.

Phillips, B. (1978). *School stress and anxiety.* New York: Human Sciences Press.

Piersel, W. C., & Kratochwill, T. R. (1979). Self-observation and behavior change: Applications to academic and adjustment problems through behavioral consultation. *Journal of School Psychology, 17,* 151–161.

Pinkston, E., Reese, N., LeBlanc, J., & Baer, D. (1973). Independent control of a preschool child's aggression and peer interaction by contingent teacher attention. *Journal of Applied Behavior Analysis, 6,* 115–124.

Platt, J. J., & Spivack, G. (1977). *Manual for Means-Ends Problem-Solving Procedure.* Philadelphia: Department of Mental Health Sciences, Hahnemann Community Mental Health/Mental Retardation Center.

Platt, J. J., Spivack, G., Altman, N., Altman, D., & Peizer, S. B. (1974). Adolescent problem solving thinking. *Journal of Consulting and Clinical Psychology, 42,* 787–793.

Platt, J. J., Spivack, G., & Bloom, M. (1971). *Means End Problem Solving Procedure (MEPS): Manual and tentative norms.* Philadelphia: Department of Health Sciences, Hahnemann Medical College and Hospital.

Porteus, S. D. (1955). *The maze test: Recent advances.* Palo Alto, CA: Pacific Books.

Putre, W., Loffio, K., Chorost, S., Marx, V., & Gilbert, C. (1977). An effectiveness study of relaxation tape with hyperactive children. *Behavior Therapy, 8,* 355–359.

Pynoos, R. S., & Nader, K. (1990). Mental health disturbances in children exposed to disaster: Prevention intervention strategies. In S. E. Goldstein, J. Yaeger, C. M. Heinicke, & R. S. Pynoos (Eds.), *Preventing mental health disturbances in children* (pp. 211–234). Washington, DC: American Psychiatric Press.

Raven, J. C. (1960). *Guide to using the Standard Progressive Matrices.* London: Lewis.

Rehm, L. D. (1977). A self-control model of depression. *Behavior Therapy, 8,* 787–804.

Reid, M. K., & Borkowski, J. G. (1987). Causal attributions of hyperactive children: Implications for teaching strategies and self-control. *Journal of Educational Psychology, 79,* 296–307.

Reynolds, W. M., & Coats, K. I. (1986). A comparison of cognitive-behavioral therapy and relaxation training for the treatment of depression in adolescents. *Journal of Consulting and Clinical Psychology, 54,* 653–660.

Reynolds, W. M., & Stark, K. D. (1986). Self-control in children: A multimethod examination of treatment outcome measures. *Journal of Abnormal Child Psychology, 14,* 13–23.

Rhode, G., Morgan, D. P., & Young, K. R. (1983). Generalization and maintenance of treatment gains of behaviorally handicapped students from resource rooms to regular classrooms using self-evaluation procedures. *Journal of Applied Behavior Analysis, 16,* 171–188.

Rhodes, W. A. (1977). Generalization of attribution re-training (Doctoral dissertation, University of Illinois at Urbana-Champaign, 1977). *Dissertation Abstracts International, 38,* 2882B.

Richter, N. C. (1984). The efficacy of relaxation training with children. *Journal of Abnormal Child Psychology, 12,* 319–344.

Robin, A., Schneider, M., & Dolnick, M. (1976). The turtle technique: An extended case study of self-control in the classroom. *Psychology in the Schools, 13,* 449–453.

Roseby, V., & Deutsch, R. (1985). Children of separation and divorce: Effects of a social role-taking group intervention on fourth and fifth graders. *Journal of Clinical Child Psychology, 14,* 55–60.

Ross, L., Rodin, J., & Zimbardo, P. G. (1969). Towards an attribution therapy. *Journal of Personality and Social Psychology, 12,* 279–288.

Rossman, H. M., & Kahnweiler, J. B. (1977). Relaxation training with intermediate grade students. *Elementary School Guidance and Counseling, 11,* 259–266.

Rotheram, M. J. (1980). Social skills training programs in elementary and high school classrooms. In D. D. Rathjen & J. P. Foreyt (Eds.), *Social competence: Intervention for children and adults* (pp. 69–112). Elmsford, NY: Pergamon.

Rotheram, M. J., Armstrong, M., & Booraem, C. (1982). Assertive training in fourth- and fifth-grade children. *American Journal of Community Psychology, 10,* 567–582.

Rotheram-Borus, M. J. (1988). Assertiveness training with children. In R. H. Price, E. L. Cowen, R. P. Lorion, & J. Ramos-McKay (Eds.), *Fourteen ounces of prevention* (pp. 83–97). Washington, DC: American Psychological Association.

Rubenstein, J. L. (1989). Suicidal behavior in "normal" adolescents: Risk and protective factors. *American Journal of Ortho-psychiatry, 59,* 59–71.

Salter, A. (1949). *Conditioned reflex therapy.* New York: Farrar, Straus & Giroux.

Santogrossi, D. A., O'Leary, K. D., Romanczyk, R. G., & Kaufman, K. F. (1973). Self-evaluation by adolescents in a psychiatric hospital school token program. *Journal of Applied Behavior Analysis, 6,* 277–287.

Sarason, I. G., & Sarason, B. R. (1981). Teaching cognitive and social skills to high school students. *Journal of Consulting and Clinical Psychology, 49,* 908–918.

Schinke, S. P. (1982). School-based model for preventing teenage pregnancy. *Social Work in Education, 4,* 34–42.

Schinke, S. P., Blythe, B. J., & Gilchrist, L. D. (1981). Cognitive-behavioral prevention of adolescent pregnancy. *Journal of Counseling Psychology, 28,* 451–454.

Schinke, S. P., & Gilchrist, L. D. (1977). Adolescent pregnancy: An interpersonal skill training approach to prevention. *Social Work in Health Care, 3,* 159–167.

Schinke, S. P., & Gilchrist, L. D. (1984). Preventing cigarette smoking with youth. *Journal of Primary Prevention, 5,* 48–53.

Schinke, S. P., Gilchrist, L. D., & Blythe, B. J. (1980). Role of communication in the prevention of teenage pregnancy. *Health and Social Work, 5,* 54–60.

Schinke, S. P., Gilchrist, L. D., & Small, R. W. (1979). Preventing unwanted adolescent pregnancy: A cognitive-behavioral approach. *American Journal of Orthopsychiatry, 49,* 81–88.

Schlichter, K. J., & Horan, J. J. (1981). Effects of stress inoculation on the anger and aggression management skills of institutionalized juvenile delinquents. *Cognitive Therapy and Research, 5,* 359–365.

Schuchman, M. C. (1977). A comparison of three techniques for reducing Scholastic Aptitude Test anxiety. *Dissertation Abstracts International, 38,* 2010.

Selye, H. (1974). *Stress without distress.* Philadelphia, PA: Lippincott.

Sharp, J., & Forman, S. G. (1985). A comparison of two approaches to anxiety management for teachers. *Behavior Therapy, 16,* 370–383.

Shure, M. B. (1980). *Interpersonal problem solving in ten-year-olds* (Final Report No. MH-27741). Washington, DC: National Institute of Mental Health.

Shure, M. B., & Spivack, G. (1972). Means-ends thinking adjustment and social class among elementary school-age children. *Journal of Consulting and Clinical Psychology, 38,* 348–353.

Shure, M. B., & Spivack, G. (1978). *Problem-solving techniques in childrearing.* San Francisco: Jossey-Bass.

Shure, M. B., & Spivack, G. (1980). Interpersonal problem-solving as a mediator of behavioral adjustment in preschool and kindergarten children. *Journal of Applied Developmental Psychology, 1,* 29–43.

Shure, M. B., & Spivack, G. (1988). Interpersonal cognitive problem solving. In R. H. Price, E. L. Cowen, R. P. Lorion, & J. Ramos-McKay (Eds.), *Fourteen ounces of prevention: A casebook for practitioners* (pp. 69–82). Washington, DC: American Psychological Association.

Shustack, B., & Fields, D. (1980). *Effects of experience and attributions on nonpersistence in children.* Paper presented at the annual meeting of the American Psychological Association, Montreal.

Silver, R. L., & Wortman, C. B. (1980). Coping with undesirable life events. In J. Garber & M.E.P. Seligman (Eds.), *Human helplessness* (pp. 279–341). San Diego, CA: Academic Press.

Smith, G. W. (1979). *A rational-emotive counseling approach to assist junior high school students with interpersonal anxiety.* Unpublished doctoral dissertation, University of Oregon.

Smith, M. S., Gad, M. T., & O'Grady, L. (1983). Psychosocial functioning, life change, and clinical status in adolescents with cystic fibrosis. *Journal of Adolescent Health Care, 4,* 230–234.

Spates, C. R., & Kanfer, F. H. (1977). Self-monitoring, self-evaluation, and self-reinforcement in children's learning: A test of a multistage self-regulation model. *Behavior Therapy, 8,* 9–16.

Spirito, A., Stark, L. J., & Williams, C. (1988). Development of a brief checklist to assess coping in pediatric populations. *Journal of Pediatric Psychology, 13,* 555–574.

Spivack, G., & Shure, M. B. (1974). *Social adjustment of young children: A cognitive approach to solving real-life problems.* San Francisco: Jossey-Bass.

Staggs, A. M. (1979). *Group counseling of learning disabled children in the intermediate grades enrolled in the public school special education program: Training in cognitive behavior modification.* Unpublished doctoral dissertation, University of Denver.

Stake, J. E., DeVille, C. J., & Pennell, C. L. (1983). The effects of assertive training on the performance self-esteem of adolescent girls. *Journal of Youth and Adolescence, 12,* 435–442.

Stark, K. D., Brookman, C. S., & Frazier, R. (1990). A comprehensive school-based treatment program for depressed children. *School Psychology Quarterly, 5,* 111–140.

Stark, K. D., Reynolds, W. M., & Kaslow, N. J. (1987). A comparison of the relative efficacy of self-control therapy and a behavioral problem-solving therapy for depression in children. *Journal of Abnormal Child Psychology, 15,* 91–113.

Stein, S. P. & Charles, E. (1971). Emotional factors in juvenile diabetes mellitus: A study of early life experiences of adolescent diabetics. *American Journal of Psychiatry, 128,* 56–60.

Sterling, S., Cowen, E. L., Weissberg, R. P., Lotyczewski, B. S., & Boike, M. (1985). Recent stressful life events and young children's social adjustment. *American Journal of Community Psychology, 13,* 87–99.

Stevens, R., & Pihl, R. (1983). Learning to cope with school: A study of the effects of a coping skill training program with test vulnerable 7th grade students. *Cognitive Therapy and Research, 1,* 155–158.

Stewart, C. G., & Lewis, W. A. (1986). Effects of assertiveness training on the self esteem of black high school students. *Journal of Counseling and Development, 64,* 638–641.

Strain, P. S. (1977). An experimental analysis of peer social initiations on the behavior of withdrawn preschool children: Some training and generalization effects. *Journal of Abnormal Child Psychology, 5,* 445–455.

Strain, P. S., Shores, R. E., & Timm, M. A. (1977). Effects of peer social initiation on the social behavior of withdrawn preschoolers. *Journal of Applied Behavior Analysis, 7*, 583–590.

Strober, M. (1984). Stressful life events associated with bulimia in anorexia nervosa. *International Journal of Eating Disorders, 3*, 1–13.

Strobino, D. (1987). Health and medical consequences. In C. Hayes & S. Hoffertn (Eds.), *Risking the future: Adolescent sexuality, pregnancy, and childbearing* (pp. 107–123). Washington, DC: National Academy Press.

Suinn, R., & Richardson, F. (1971). Anxiety management training: A nonspecific behavior therapy program for anxiety control. *Behavior Therapy, 2*, 498–510.

Tanner, V. L., & Holliman, W. B. (1988). Effectiveness of assertiveness training in modifying aggressive behaviors of young children. *Psychological Reports, 62*, 39–46.

Thomas, A. (1989). Ability and achievement expectations: Implications of research for classroom practice. *Childhood Education, 65*, 235–241.

Thomas, A., & Pashley, B. (1982). Effects of classroom training on LD students' task persistence and attributions. *Learning Disability Quarterly, 5*, 133–144.

Tisdelle, D. A., & St. Lawrence, J. S. (1986). Interpersonal problem-solving competency: Review and critique of the literature. *Clinical Psychology Review, 6*, 337–356.

Tobler, N. S. (1986). Meta-analysis of 143 adolescent drug prevention programs: Quantitative outcome results of program participants compared to a control or comparison group. *Journal of Drug Issues, 16*, 537–567.

Turk, D. (1975). *Cognitive control of pain: A skills training approach for the treatment of pain*. Unpublished master's thesis, University of Waterloo.

Turk, D., Meichenbaum, D., & Genest, M. (1983). *Pain and behavioral medicine*. New York: Guilford.

Vacc, N. A., & Greenleaf, S. M. (1980). Relaxation training and covert positive reinforcement with elementary school children. *Elementary School Guidance and Counseling, 14*, 232–235.

Valins, S., & Nisbett, R. E. (1971). *Some implications of attribution processes for the development and treatment of emotional disorders.* New York: General Learning Press.

Vogrin, D., & Kassinove, H. (1979). Effects of behavior rehearsal, audiotaped observation, and intelligence on assertiveness and adjustment in third-grade children. *Psychology in the Schools, 16,* 422–429.

Vygotsky, L. S. (1962). *Thought and language.* New York: Wiley.

Waksman, S. A. (1984). Assertion training with adolescents. *Adolescence, 73,* 123–130.

Walker, H. M. (1983). *Walker Problem Behavior Identification Checklist: Test and manual* (2nd ed.). Los Angeles: Western Psychological Services.

Walker, H. M., & McConnell, S. (1988). *Scale of Social Competence and School Adjustment.* Austin, TX: Pro-Ed.

Wall, S. M. (1982). Effects of systematic self-monitoring and self-reinforcement in children's management of test performances. *Journal of Psychology, 111,* 129–136.

Warren, R., Deffenbacher, J. L., & Brading, P. (1976). Rational-emotive therapy and the reduction of text anxiety in elementary school students. *Rational Living, 11,* 26–29.

Waters, V. (1981). The living school. *RET Work, 1,* 1–6.

Waters, V. (1982). Therapies for children: Rational emotive therapy. In C. R. Reynolds & T. B. Gutkin (Eds.), *Handbook of school psychology* (pp. 570–579). New York: Wiley.

Watson, D. L., & Tharp, R. G. (1985). *Self-directed behavior: Self modification for personal adjustment.* Monterey, CA: Brooks/Cole.

Wechsler, D. (1949). *Manual: Wechsler Intelligence Scale for Children.* New York: Psychological Corporation.

Wehr, S. H., & Kaufman, M. E. (1987). The effects of assertive training on performance in higher anxious adolescents. *Adolescence, 22,* 195–205.

Weiner, B. (1972). Attribution theory, achievement motivation, and the educational process. *Review of Educational Research, 42,* 203–215.

Weiner, B. (1979). A theory of motivation for some classroom experiences. *Journal of Educational Psychology, 71,* 3–25.

Westoff, C. F., Calcot, G., & Foster, A. D. (1983). Teenage fertility in developed nations. *Family Planning Perspectives, 15,* 105.

Whalen, C., Henker, B., & Henshaw, S. (1985). Cognitive-behavioral therapies for hyperactive children: Premises, problems, and prospects. *Journal of Abnormal Child Psychology, 13,* 391–410.

Whitehill, M. B., Hersen, M., & Bellack, A. S. (1980). Conversation skills training for socially isolated children. *Behavior Research and Therapy, 18,* 217–225.

Wielkiewicz, R. M. (1986). *Behavior management in the schools: Principles and procedures.* Elmsford, NY: Pergamon.

Wills, T. A. (1986). Stress and coping in early adolescence: Relationships to substance use in urban school samples. *Health Psychology, 5,* 503–529.

Witt, J. C., & Elliott, S. N. (1985). Acceptability of classroom management strategies. In T. R. Kratochwill (Ed.), *Advances in school psychology* (Vol. 4, pp. 251–288). Hillsdale, NJ: Erlbaum.

Wolf, M. M. (1978). Social validity: The case for subjective measurement or how applied behavior analysis is finding its heart. *Journal of Applied Behavior Analysis, 11,* 203–214.

Wolpe, J. (1958). *Psychotherapy by reciprocal inhibition.* Stanford, CA: Stanford University Press.

Wolpe, J. (1962). The experimental foundations of some new psychotherapeutic methods. In A. J. Bachrach (Ed.), *Experimental foundations of clinical psychology* (pp. 554–575). New York: Basic Books.

Wolpe, J., & Lazarus, A. A. (1966). *Behavior therapy techniques.* Elmsford, NY: Pergamon.

Wood, R., & Michelson, L. (1978). *Children's assertive behavior scales.* Unpublished manuscript.

Workman, E. A. (1982). *Teaching behavioral self-control to students.* Austin, TX: Pro-Ed.

Wright, J. (1978). An investigation of the effectiveness of a relaxation training model on discipline referrals. *Dissertation Abstracts International, 39,* 2162.

Zieffle, T. H., & Romney, D. M. (1985). Comparison of self-instruction and relaxation training in reducing impulsive and inattentive behavior of learning disabled children on cognitive tasks. *Psychological Reports, 57,* 271-274.

Zins, J. E., & Forman, S. G. (1988). Primary prevention in the schools: What are we waiting for? *School Psychology Review, 17,* 539-541.

# Name Index

# Subject Index

## A

Adjustment, and social problem solving, 45

Administrators, and implementation, 157–158, 160–161

Adolescent Assertion Expression Scale (AAES), 71–72

Adolescent Perceived Events Scale (APES), 7, 9

Aggression: assertiveness training for, 74–75; inoculation training for, 114–115; self-instruction training for, 83, 89; social skills training for, 61–62

AIDS, prevention programs for, 151–152

Alcohol and other drug abuse: assertiveness training for, 76; prevention programs for, 146–149

Alternative behaviors reinforcement (ALT-R), for social skills, 62

Anger control, stress inoculation for, 113–115

Anxiety: assertiveness training for, 75; stress inoculation for, 115–116

Anxiety management: in prevention program, 148; for stress, 105

Appraisal, primary and secondary, 4

Assertiveness training: aspects of, 64–78; assessment instruments

for, 70–72; and cultural diversity, 77–78; defined, 64–65; development of, 65–66; in prevention programs, 147, 148, 150, 151; procedures for, 66–70; research on, 72–77; summary on, 77–78; theme- or exercise-oriented, 67–68

Attribution retraining: aspects of, 117–128; assessment instruments for, 123–124; defined, 117–118; development of, 118–119; procedures for, 119–123; research on, 125–127; summary on, 127–128

## B

Behavior disorders, self-instruction training for, 89–90

Behavior rehearsal, in social skills training, 53

Behavioral Assertiveness Test for Children (BAT-C), 72

Behavioral diaries, for self-observation, 132

Behavioral self-management training: aspects of, 129–144; defined, 129; development of, 130–131; multicomponent programs for, 142–144; procedures for, 131–137; research on, 137–144; summary on, 144

Breathing, deep, 33